P
*We Bought*

*"When Americans were called upon ............... ~~...~~wing the 1941 Pearl Harbor attack, the students of South High School in Grand Rapids, Mich., did more than their share with their contribution to the 1942 'Buy a Bomber' campaign. Writing in the simple, unadorned terms of small-town America during wartime, Warren, a writer from the South High class of 1962, captures the patriotism and community spirit that sparked the students to canvass door-to-door. She chronicles the eager pupils who raised more than $75,000 in sales of war bonds and Defense Loan stamps in order to buy a fighter plane. The drive continued to bring in donations and the students subsequently collected more than $300,000 to purchase a B-17 bomber, which was named The Spirit of South High. (Unfortunately, the bomber crashed in a farmer's field during a training mission in bad weather.) Warren honors the school leadership, students, and local merchants with lofty praise, while noting some additional government support. This bit of local history is a reminder of unheralded resolve and determination by students during WWII."*

— *Publishers Weekly/BookLife*

*"I read Sandra's book. It is well written and researched. I recommend it for the history, the human faces and stories, and the superb writing."*
— *Julie Murphy, Ph.D. Licensed Professional Counselor*

*"...You have published this book at a time in life when our national spirit is low...Maybe this book will help ignite 'I'm proud to be an American!'"*
— *Sallee Wiltrakis Ballard, SHS Class of 1962*

*"Thank you for writing We Bought A WWII Bomber. I gave it to my 95-year old father for his birthday. The book prompted him to speak of his WWII experiences for the first time. My brother and I sat mesmerized for over two hours amazed to learn all he had lived through."*
— *Bruce Fisher, Son of a WWII Veteran*

*"I was a nine year old child in London in 1944 and my family and friends all thought Americans had lots of extra food because they sent it to us. We, the English, were starving because of the German U-boat raids. I'm shocked to learn that Americans sacrificed so that we could eat!"*
— *Frederick Hardy, Charlotte, NC*

# WE BOUGHT A
# WWII BOMBER

The Untold Story of

A Michigan High School

a B-17 Bomber

& The Blue Ridge Parkway!

SANDRA WARREN
Arlie Enterprises

Other Military Books by Sandra Warren

When Duty Called:
Even Grandma Had to Go

Hidden Casualties:
Battles on the Homefront

Find these and other books at:
www.arliebooks.com

Library of Congress Control Number: 2015910895
Historical Non-Fiction/Memoir/Biography
Cover design: Books That Matter www.kimberlyrae.com/booksthatmatter
Front cover photo - Courtesy of The Grand Rapids Public Museum.

Unless otherwise credited, interior photos are courtesy of Grand Rapids History &
Special Collections, Archives, Grand Rapids Public Library, Grand Rapids,
Michigan
ISBN-978-1880175-06-4
Revised Edition, 2016
Printed in the United States of America

# DEDICATION

This book is dedicated with love, admiration and great respect to the students attending South High School in 1943, the teachers who supported them and the brave men who piloted and were crew members flying *The Spirit of South High*. All exemplified the reason Tom Brokaw called the people living during that era, "The Greatest Generation!"

# TABLE OF CONTENTS

# FOREWORD BY DAVID DUTCHER

*Co-chairing the South High Bond Campaign turned out to be a life-changing opportunity for me. Spearheading this effort during my sophomore, junior, and seniors years was the the highlight of my high school experience and inspired me to civil service for many years to come. Persuading the 1,500 member student body to sell war bonds and stamps, to boost the war effort, was easy. During the next 50 years I followed South High's teaching moments: Find a worthy project and get it done.*

*David Dutcher, JD, MBA*
*University of Michigan*
*52 years Michigan Attorney*
*"Buy a Bomber" Co-Chairman*

# FOREWORD BY MAJOR ARVAL STREADBECK

*Sandra Warren takes us on a fascinating journey through the years, regarding South High School and B-17 bomber number 42-29577.*

*I am so impressed with the patriotism of the students of South High School and the surrounding communities, and in-turn, appreciative of the marvelous support the "home teams everywhere" provided for all the troops on the "front lines." Her book has also re-kindled my fondness and appreciation for the good people in Meadows of Dan and Willis, Virginia, who were so kind, helpful, and pleasant when a group of young airmen…literally "dropped in" unexpectedly. They have my enduring gratitude.*

*Major Arval Louis Streadbeck*
*Airplane Commander & Instructor,*
*"The Spirit of South High"*
*99-years young*

# PREFACE

The story within the pages of this book was begging to be told. What started as casual conversation with old classmates grew into the retelling of a remarkable event that began in the lives of school children during WWII and didn't end until the year 2015, seventy-two years later. This labor of love continued to grow as each interview, each revelation, each fact I explored increased my respect and awe of the individuals involved. I've never engaged in any other writing project that has given me such pleasure.

Sandra Dieleman Warren
South High School Class of 1962

SANDRA WARREN

# PART ONE

# *THE SCHOOL*

South High School

Grand Rapids, Michigan

Chapter One
# WWII Home Front

World War II began in Europe in 1939, although it wasn't until the day after the Japanese attack on Pearl Harbor on December 7, 1941, the United States of America officially entered the war. That act of aggression galvanized the citizens of the United States to action. From the Atlantic to the Pacific, big city to the tiniest mountain hollow, Americans became invested in the war effort wanting to do their part.

Overnight the need for materials to make military equipment, uniforms and protective gear exploded as did the need for food to feed the hordes of Americans who enlisted or were drafted to serve. By the end of the war, the cost of those materials would exceed two hundred ninety-five billion dollars.[1] "Fifty-seven percent of the cost not covered by taxes was obtained by borrowing directly from American citizens through the sale of government bonds. Americans viewed bond purchases as their patriotic duty..."[2]

Through newspapers, magazines, newsreels between shows at the local theater, and on street corners, advertisements began to appear. Posters implored men and women to "do your part" and "join the fight" by enlisting or conserving in a variety of ways: car-pooling to save gas and rubber, planting Victory Gardens to make up for empty shelves in the grocery stores, buying war bonds to help finance the war and salvaging scrap: metals, paper, rubber and rags. "It's your duty," the posters proclaimed.

*Courtesy of Collections Smithsonian Institute, Washington, DC*

With multiple items critical to the war effort identified each town established drop-off locations, often in school yards, for collecting the goods. Folks young and old saved paper, not just old newspapers, magazines and cardboard, but wrapping paper and old letters as well. They reclaimed rubber from old tires, inner tubes, hot water bottles, old sink mats, bath mats, bathing caps and even rubber bathing suits. The rubber was remade into parts for military equipment and clothing. Four Army coats could be made from the rubber in a fifty-foot garden hose. There was an urgent need for cast-off clothing, handkerchiefs, sheets, towels, sugar sacks and burlap bags to make rags for cleaning tools and machinery in thousands of machine shops and on tanks, airplanes and ships. Old draperies and carpets went into roofing and flooring for emergency construction. Scrap metal, steel, aluminum and tin made military equipment and other implements necessary for war. Women even turned in their excess pots and pans from their kitchens.[3]

Food rationing became necessary to feed the growing numbers of troops. Americans understood and didn't complain when meat, sugar, fish, fats and cheeses became scarce and required a food stamp for purchase. Even a pair of shoes required a stamp. Victory Gardens popped up and citizens shared their bounty. When gas was rationed for nonessential drivers, those not driving to and from jobs that forwarded the war effort, folks car-pooled. American women volunteered to work in the factories and their husbands and sons went to war. Adults and children bought War Bonds and Defense Stamps. American flags flew proudly from businesses, churches and homes, and Gold Stars hung in windows, a sad sign that family members had paid the ultimate price for their country.

Country-wide salvage programs began and teachers, parents and children played a vital role. Scrap drives and salvage drives between communities and organizations became a new competitive sport. Schools, home rooms, different grade levels, academic and sports clubs vied to see which group could bring in the most tin cans, aluminum or keys, whatever was the focus of the particular drive.

Teachers held scrap drives and sold War Stamps in their classrooms. Students purchased a War Stamp for either ten cents or twenty-five cents and then pasted them into individual War Stamp Books. The cost of stamps to fill a book was eighteen dollars and seventy-five cents. Once filled, the child exchanged the stamp book for a War Bond redeemed for twenty-five dollars when held to maturity, initially a period of fixed ten years.

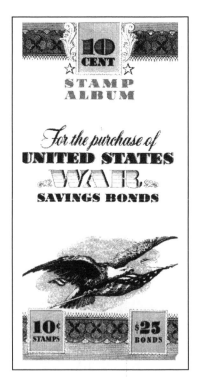

*Courtesy of Sandra Warren*

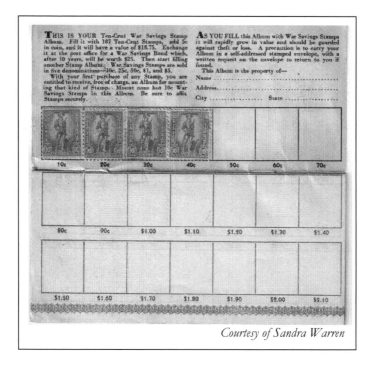

THIS IS YOUR Ten-Cent War Savings Stamp Album. Fill it with 187 Ten-Cent Stamps, add 5c in coin, and it will have a value of $18.75. Exchange it at the post office for a War Savings Bond which, after 10 years, will be worth $25. Then start filling another Stamp Album. War Savings Stamps are sold in five denominations—10c, 25c, 50c, $1, and $5.

With your first purchase of any Stamp, you are entitled to receive, free of charge, an Album for mounting that kind of Stamp. Mount none but 10c War Savings Stamps in this Album. Be sure to affix Stamps securely.

AS YOU FILL this Album with War Savings Stamps it will rapidly grow in value and should be guarded against theft or loss. A precaution is to carry your Album in a self-addressed stamped envelope, with a written request on the envelope to return to you if found.

This Album is the property of—

Name ........................................
Address ........................................
City .................. State ..................

| 10c | 20c | 30c | 40c | 50c | 60c | 70c |

| 80c | 90c | $1.00 | $1.10 | $1.20 | $1.30 | $1.40 |

| $1.50 | $1.60 | $1.70 | $1.80 | $1.90 | $2.00 | $2.10 |

*Courtesy of Sandra Warren*

The selling and buying of War Stamps taught children from first grade through junior high valuable lessons in arithmetic, money-management and savings. Students also learned the more important reality of being good citizens, doing their parts to help fathers or brothers or uncles in the military to win and end the war.[4]

The popular educational resources used in schools throughout the country, *My Weekly Reader: The Children's Newspaper* for younger grades and *My Weekly Reader: The Junior Newspaper* for junior high students carried numerous suggestions to involve students in the war effort under titles such as, "Uncle Sam Needs Boys & Girls"[5] and "Children Can Help"[6] This weekly newspaper brought the realities of war down to a child's level of understanding through articles and activities.

Chapter Two
# The War Impacts South High


World War II changed schools drastically and South High's seventh through twelfth grade school located on the south side of Grand Rapids, Michigan was no exception. Well integrated for most of its twenty-nine years, South High's student body mushroomed as people of all races moved north to work in factories converted to the war effort. [7]

While the student population increased, materials needed to operate South High became limited. Shortages demanded adjustments in all aspects of school life. Janitors were forced to cut back on polishing floors as floor oils and cleaning fluids became scarce. Thermostats were turned down during the colder months and kept at a range of sixty-eight to seventy degrees with orders to double up in some classes if radiators should break. Rubber parts to repair radiators were impossible to obtain.

The paper shortage forced teachers to assign lessons that would only take one page to complete. Penny pencils were no longer being made, forcing students to pay more for their writing instruments. Erasers, paper clips and rubber bands were hard to get.

In sewing class, girls made dickeys—detachable shirt collars worn under other garments—out of their brothers' shirts and skirts out of old trousers. Because zippers and hooks-and-eyes were unavailable, students created fashions using buttonholes.

Shortages of oranges, sugar and meats forced teachers in the food classes to be creative and innovative. They developed multiple recipes using meat-extenders such as rice and cheese to make up for the lack of meat. Grease from cooking classes was saved to be reused for making glycerin, an ingredient in ammunition.

By January, 1943, typewriters were no longer being produced so when the government expressed a need for them for their offices, the typing class donated four. [8]

All classroom teachers were encouraged to collect materials that otherwise would have been thrown out. Art classes collected empty paint tubes. The cafeteria saved grease, fats used in seasoning, bones and old tin cans. The shop and woodworking classes assigned smaller projects to conserve on wood and diminish waste by finding uses for the scraps.[9]

By government order all copper and zinc printing plates unused for at least a year had to be turned in. The *Tattler* school newspaper staff and the *Spectra* yearbook staff disposed of hundreds of engravings used in these two publications; copper from the yearbook engravings and zinc from the newspaper "cuts." Boys from woodshop classes pried the engravings from the hardwood printing blocks to which they were nailed and then sorted them.[10]

Projects in South's wood-working classes changed focus from desks and bread boards to war effort projects designed according to Government Issue. One such project was to make model airplanes for the Navy using plans sent out by the U.S. Navy Bureau of Aeronautics. The work required accuracy because the model airplanes were to be used to train military and civilian pilots and airplane spotters to quickly recognize all aspects of airplanes flying for both the Allies and Axis countries.

Shop boys also learned repair and maintenance of South's machines. They made chisels, gears, punches, squares and centers making sure to save materials no longer available. [11]

When South students participated in a city-wide scrap drive for metals of all kinds, the decision was made to sacrifice old sports trophies, won in hard-fought battles, to the cause. Principal Sherman Coryell, and teachers Mr. Henry Mulder and Mr. LeValley set an example by donating prized World War I souvenirs including German helmets.

Activity classes during the final period of the day were expanded to include sessions on first aid, block mother assistants, caring for children whose parents were working in the factories and nursery school training.

As the years wore on school cafeteria managers were constantly making adjustments. In addition to rationing becoming more severe, the amount of food consumed in the cafeteria the previous spring determined the allotted rationing points for the current year. Even though there were twice as many students buying lunches in 1943 as in the previous year, the food allotment was approximately one-third of what was needed. [12]

Rationing prompted one student in 1943 to write a poem that was published in December 23rd issue of *The South High Tattler*, the school's newspaper. Little did she know that it would be almost two years before the sentiment in the last line would come true.

## Rationing
### by Nan Gilders

Peaches, pears, and all things canned
    From the market have been banned.
If you're driving with "A" stamp gas
    No one on the road you'll pass.
If you have no points for meat,
    Cheese will soon become a treat;
And if you go with feet all bare
    People have no right to stare.
I heard that hamburger was raised today
    To eight points by the O.P.A.
If you miss cheese, meat and butter,
    You have no real excuse to sputter
For, in spite of all the worry
    The war will end in more of a hurry.[13]

Although the junior high population was growing, 1943 recorded its smallest senior class in twenty-two years, a direct result of the war. Schools all over the city reported similar patterns. More and more young men left school to enlist. But another phenomenon also occurred. Those students who worked summer jobs in defense factories made good wages, and were reluctant to give them up in the fall to return to school.[14]

Chapter Three
# The Instigator

In the Fall of 1942, students filed into Mr. Mulder's eighth grade Civics classroom at South High School, unaware that an event that would go down in school history was about to be initiated by none other than Arthur Blackport, one of the quietest students in the room.

Arthur took his seat in the back row next to his friend Mel Hartger as Mr. Mulder passed out the latest issue of *My Weekly Reader, The Junior Newspaper.* The entire class was to read the issue together and discuss each article.

On this day, Mr. Mulder began by pointing to the blackboard where he had written the numbers of military guns, ships and planes needed in 1943 to help the fighting soldiers. He referenced a chart found in a 1942 issue of *My Weekly Reader* that called for the production of thirty-five thousand anti-aircraft guns, seventy-five thousand tanks and one hundred and twenty-five thousand planes. "If all the needed airplanes were stored in the same airport at the same time," Mr. Mulder read, "the airport alone would have to be over 250 miles long."[15]

# MY WEEKLY READER

**EDITION NUMBER FIVE . . .**

**. . . THE JUNIOR NEWSPAPER**

EDITORIAL BOARD: DRS. WILLIAM S. GRAY, ARTHUR I. GATES, GERALD YOAKAM, ERNEST HORN, PAUL WITTY, EMMETT BETTS

| Vol. XX | Week of February 16-20, 1942 | No. 22 |

## America Shows What It Can Do

| | 1941 | 1942 | 1943 |
|---|---|---|---|
| PLANES | 19,000 | 60,000 40,000 Combat | 125,000 100,000 Combat |
| TANKS | 7500 | 45,000 | 75,000 |
| GUNS (Anti-Aircraft) | 3000 | 20,000 | 35,000 |
| SHIPS (Merchant Vessels) | 1,100,000 TONS | 8,000,000 TONS | 10,800,000 TONS |

This chart outlines part of America's work for the next two years.

THINK of some place that is about 120 miles from where you live. Then imagine a giant airport as long as that distance and one mile wide. An airport that big would be needed to hold all the warplanes that America will build during the year 1942. The airplanes would have to be placed as close together as possible.

An airport to hold the warplanes America will build next year (1943) would have to be more than 250 miles long. During 1942 and 1943, 185,000 warplanes will be built. That many of anything can hardly be imagined.

This year and next, America will build swarms of warplanes. Building warplanes is only a small part of the work America will do, however. The chart shows how many tanks, antiaircraft guns, and ships will be built. America will build a warplane every four minutes, a tank every seven minutes, and two ships a day. The time you spend reading this story is enough to finish several airplanes or a large part of a ship.

Even the work shown on the chart is only a small part of the war work America will do. Thousands of army trucks must be made. There must be tons of ammunition. There must be food and clothing for the soldiers. There must be medicines and bandages. You can think of many other kinds of work that must be done by America at war.

Work in the amount planned has never before been done by any nation. America has never done so much before, but all Americans know that they can do what has been asked.

In order to do this work, we must make changes in our way of living and in our way of doing things. For years, America has been a peaceful nation, living in peaceful ways. It cannot change to a nation at war without making changes in Americans' ways of living.

Some of these changes have already come. More will follow. The making of automobiles has stopped. We need airplanes and tanks now more than we need new automobiles. Automobile factories are being changed to airplane and tank factories.

In a short time, the making of new radios for home use will be cut almost in half. Our fighters need more radio equipment. Some of the materials used in ordinary radios are needed as war materials. Rubber, tin, and aluminum have become almost precious. They are being saved for only the most important uses. Men's suits will be made with less material. Eleven suits will be made of the same amount of material now being used for ten. We must all be more saving of everything.

One man is in charge of all America's war work. You can see how important his job is. He is Donald Marr Nelson. The President placed Mr. Nelson in charge of the Nation's war work a few weeks ago. Mr. Nelson's job is to speed up our war work and to keep it going.

Mr. Nelson is a good man for this job. He has had years of experience in getting things done in

Meet Donald M. Nelson. He is "boss" of America's war work. He works hard, too — from early in the morning until late at night. His home is near Chicago.

Manufacturing all this equipment would take millions and millions of dollars. "Everyone has to do his part," Mr. Mulder said, as he passed out the new copies of *My Weekly Reader*.

Featured on the cover of the new issue was an article about the "Buy a Bomber" campaign. Cities, businesses, organizations, even schools could contribute to the purchase of individual aircraft by selling War Bonds and War Loan Stamps, the article proclaimed. Once purchased, the plane would be named by the group, and flown into a local airport for a dedication ceremony.

Shouts of disbelief were heard as everyone started talking at once.

"Quiet down. Let's continue," Mr. Mulder said as he turned back to the newspaper at hand.

The amount of War Bonds sold determined the type of aircraft purchased; seventy-five thousand dollars bought a pursuit fighter or a tiny liaison plane converted for medivac duties. One hundred ten thousand dollars funded a twin engine B-25, and for selling three hundred thousand dollars of War Bonds, a B-24 or B-17 Flying Fortress could be purchased.[16]

Excitement that had been mounting ceased after Mr. Mulder read the cost of each aircraft. Silence permeated the room. Then, from the back row a hand shot up. It was Arthur Blackport, never-raise-your-hand, Arthur.

"Mr. Mulder," he said, "why don't we do that?"[17]

Chapter Four
# Igniting the Campaign

Things moved quickly after Arthur asked his question. Mr. Mulder sent him, along with his friend Mel, to the office of the principal, Mr. Sherman Coryell, who wholeheartedly endorsed the idea. When presented to the Senior Student Council, high school juniors, David Dutcher and Grace Moyer stepped forward to co-chair the campaign. Ruth Ann Jenkins offered to be secretary. The committee retained eighth graders, Arthur Blackport and Mel Hartger as co-chairmen for having been the instigators.

Arthur Blackport

Mel Hartger

| Mr. Sherman Coryell, Principal | Mr. Henry Mulder |

| David Dutcher | Grace Moyer | Ruth Ann Jenkins |

*Courtesy of 1943 & 1944 South High School Spectras*

Harry Brown, a 1923 graduate of South High and the chairman of the Kent County Retailers' War Savings Committee, met with Mr. Mulder and the new committee to share organizational strategies. This campaign to buy a war plane was to be the greatest single-purpose drive in the history of the school and needed specialized guidance. [18]

Mr. Brown refined the method already in place for selling War Loan Stamps to bring in pledges for War Bond purchases. Mr. Mulder compiled two thousand circulars explaining the campaign with directions to fill out a bond application. The circulars identified three locations near the school willing to accept the applications: nearby Union Bank, Four Star Theater and the South High School Bookstore. School treasurer, Mr. Lee Newton, would certify South High Bookstore sales to the war savings staff. Customers purchasing bonds at off-school locations were to request credit be given to the "South High School 'Buy a Bomber' Campaign." [19]

Like established books of War Loan Stamps, War Bonds for this purpose were at seventy-five percent of face value. A one hundred dollar bond cost seventy-five dollars. Bonds were available in increments of twenty-five dollars up to two hundred dollars, then skipping to five hundred, one thousand and five thousand. [20]

The "Buy a Bomber" committee chose the purchase of a small pursuit fighter plane as the focus of the campaign. Sales of seventy-five thousand dollars in War Loan Stamps and War Bonds were needed to meet that goal. Optimistically, the committee believed the campaign could be accomplished in approximately three months' time and set April 1, 1943 as the end date of the campaign.

Students painted a large mural of a fighter plane along with the seventy-five thousand dollar price tag and the ending date. The poster was to be displayed in the lower front corridor under the painting of the school, following the official announcement of the campaign.[21]

*Courtesy of South High School Spectra*

In mid-December, 1942, two assemblies announced the campaign to South High's sixteen hundred students, one for the junior high student body and one for the senior high. Dave Dutcher, student Co-chairman of the campaign, standing next to the painted poster, opened both events with a rousing speech. Mr. Brown, from the War Savings Committee, and Mr. Mulder followed explaining how each student could help.

Following the presentations, enthusiasm and excitement for the campaign exploded. The entire student body, along with teachers, then became one gigantic force. Gone were the individual class salvage drives, club efforts and competitions between home rooms. All had been replaced with a singular purpose, "Buy that plane." The spirit of South High, lying dormant deep within each student, burst into action.

Word spread fast. This goal was tangible. There was no need to wonder where donated money was going. A fighter plane, emblazoned with *The Spirit of South High,* could directly affect the outcome of the war. South High Students were buying a fighter plane and most everyone wanted to be a part of it.

Co-Chairmen David Dutcher and Grace Moyer selling War Loan Stamps in the hallway of South High School.
*Courtesy of 1944 South High School Spectra*

Clubs and organizations within school first completed drives already in place and then refocused their energies toward the "Buy a Bomber" drive. On Wednesday, December 16, 1942, during seventh hour, classmates who purchased a War Loan Stamp could attend a student sponsored "Buy a Bomber Entertainment Show" featuring singers, an accordion player, instrumentalists, dancers and acrobats. The price of admission brought in nearly two hundred dollars. Organizers of the Yule Jump, the annual Christmas dance, added a silent auction with merchandise donated by local merchants. The highest bidder was required to purchase a War Bond.[22]

Unleashed on the community, students put advertisements in local stores and nearby theaters, and canvassed friends and residents in South High neighborhoods. They went from house to house and the local merchants. Students worked odd jobs to earn money. They emptied their piggy-banks. Working parents approached employers and colleagues for donations. From dimes that purchased War Loan Stamps one at a time to War Bonds worth thousands, the money dribbled in slowly.

On January 8, 1943, three and a half weeks into the campaign, Mr. Newton reported that in order to meet their goal to buy that fighter plane, students would have to bring in six thousand dollars a week for the next twelve weeks. He encouraged students to talk to everyone they knew. He cited stories, from two teachers, Miss Goss and one from Mr. Mulder. Both admitted to having lost out on significant War Bond sales credit because they failed to tell a relative and a friend about giving South credit before bonds were purchased.

Mr. Newton's sales report rekindled a flame under the student body. They responded by bringing in the funds. A little more than four weeks later, a mere two months after the campaign began, it was over. The goal to raise seventy-five thousand dollars selling War Bonds and War Stamps was achieved. The students of South High school had their fighter plane.

*The Spirit of South High School,* North American Texan Advanced Trainer, AT-6A, with Miss South High, Queen LaVonne Kronberg with Jean Endsley, Velma Kling, Lucille Hice, Barbara Northway, Margaret McCarthy

Harry Brown returned to the school to congratulate the "Buy a Bomber" committee and to watch as Mr. Mulder pasted a large "Paid to Uncle Sam" sign on the poster of the plane.

Mr. Henry Mulder adds PAID to the "Buy a Bomber" campaign sign.

*Courtesy of South High School Spectra*

The students of South High School accomplished their goal, yet the credit for more bond sales kept rolling in. This motivated the committee to greater heights. If they raised seventy-five thousand dollars for a small fighter plane so quickly, members rationalized, could three hundred thousand dollars more for a B-17 Flying Fortress bomber be that difficult? The committee wanted to try. Mr. Mulder and Mr. Newton agreed, restating the importance of the on-going war effort and that students had a duty to continue contributions. The "Buy a Bomber" committee set its sights on raising three-hundred thousand dollars more.

Students painted another poster; this one showing a B-17 Flying Fortress in flight along with the three hundred thousand dollar price tag. Instead of replacing the original poster, they decided the large 'paid' sign pasted next to the fighter plane served as a visual incentive. The newly painted poster updating the campaign was attached underneath.

The new goal. Students grouped around the poster are left to right, Mary Toarmina, Ruth Ann Jenkins, Chester Ward, Mel Hartger, Jim Seino with Arthur Blackport, initiator of the "Buy a Bomber" campaign, on the ladder.

Harry Brown returned to meet with the student body a second time at an assembly on February 12th and launched the campaign to raise an additional three hundred thousand dollars to buy a B-17, Flying Fortress bomber. The assembly opened with the entire student body singing patriotic songs. A student read a poem he'd written dedicated to boys overseas. A skit was performed by the dramatics class, the Glee Club sang and the band played. Introduced during the event were a nurse, two gray ladies (women who worked for the Red Cross), a soldier, a sailor and a marine. The marine, wounded at Guadalcanal, spoke about the importance of what the students were doing. The assembly ended with David Dutcher leading the student body in a rousing cheer for the campaign. [23]

This time the campaign would be more wide-spread than the first, extending to the entire south side of Grand Rapids to its merchants and businesses. The potential for success was great with this added involvement of approximately one quarter of Grand Rapids' one hundred sixty-four thousand residents.[24] Additional banks had come on board during the final push of the previous campaign providing more locations where bonds could be purchased in the name of the South High School Bomber campaign.

Like a bomber preparing for take-off, once the War Bond sales revved up, pledges began to roll in faster and faster. The amount of money paid out for bonds in South's name astounded the advisors, Dave Dutcher and the committee. Within two weeks, the end was in sight.

On February 23, 1943, the campaign committee sponsored an evening event that became the climax of the campaign. That event, "The South High Bomber-for-Victory," featured a skit performed by the Thespians, "The Dollar Bill Talks," written by Robert Gray. Fifteen hundred patrons each paid the cost of a twenty-five-dollar War Bond to attend, bringing in nearly thirty-eight-thousand dollars in one evening. [25]

By the end of February, far ahead of the April first deadline, what once seemed impossible was accomplished. Through the sale of War Bonds, South High School students, with the support of faculty, family, local merchants and the Grand Rapids community raised the extraordinary sum of three hundred thousand dollars. Yet that wasn't the end of the campaign. Reports of War Bonds purchased in the name of South High's "Buy a Bomber" campaign continued, and by christening day, three hundred seventy-five thousand dollars had been credited to the school. The B-17 Flying Fortress bomber was theirs to name.

It would be called, *The Spirit of South High.*

Chapter Five
# The Christening

Word spread quickly of the success of the "Buy a Bomber" campaign. Plans for what would become known as "Bomber Day" were in full swing when a letter arrived stating that a representative of the Secretary of the United States Treasury was coming to South High to honor those responsible for the success of the campaign.

Mr. Walter J. Wade arrived a few days later and spoke at an assembly honoring Mr. Mulder and the "Buy a Bomber" campaign committee. He presented Mr. Mulder with a Distinguished Service Citation made out to South High School for its successful bomber campaign. Mr. Wade also awarded Minute Man Badge lapel pins to the four Co-Chairmen, Dave Dutcher, Grace Moyer, Arthur Blackport and Mel Hartger, along with campaign Secretary Ruth Ann Jenkins.

Mr. Wade's visit prompted the junior and senior high Student Council to create an award of their own. To thank Mr. Mulder for all his hard work, they surprised him with "Mulder Day" placing with a large block letter "M" on walls in the corridors to thank him for all his diligent efforts.

Mr. Mulder shows award from the United States Treasury Department to Art Blackport, Mel Hartger, Grace Moyer, Dave Dutcher and Ruth Ann Jenkins

*Courtesy of South High School Spectra*

The bomber committee and the Student Council also honored elementary students who had participated in the "Buy a Bomber" campaign. The South High School concert band traveled to six of the eight feeder schools and presented special assemblies. Students from two additional elementary schools walked to South High for the program. Each elementary school principal received a citation for their schools' contribution to the campaign. [26]

Presentation of the awards and citations at all the assemblies enhanced excitement for the upcoming "Bomber Day." The celebration was to be held on April 6, 1943, Army Day, the twenty-sixth anniversary of the entrance of the United States into World War I. Early dismissal of school would free students and faculty members to join a huge parade led by South High's marching band in full uniform. The committee invited grade school students and interested community members to join the parade. All participants were encouraged to wear patriotic costumes and the school colors, red and blue of South High School.

On the appointed day, students gathered at Garfield Park, a nearby playground, and took their places in the parade to march to the Kent County airport, two miles away. The school band led the procession followed by two companies of South High ROTC troops. Three Army jeeps came next, one carrying the Bomber Queen, LaVonne Kronberg and her attendants, the second holding Co-Chairmen Arthur Blackport and Mel Hartger, the originators of the campaign, and in the third, bomber committee officers Co-Chairman Grace Moyer and Secretary Ruth Ann Jenkins along with "Buy a Bomber" Campaign Advisor, Mr. Mulder. Co-Chairman Dave Dutcher was slated to ride in one of the jeeps but he chose instead to honor his commitment to the band where he played trombone. A float, depicting the Allied nations and created by the Senior Class, preceded groups of students marching with their respective classes. Grade school students and neighborhood children, riding decorated bicycles brought up the end of the parade.

South "On Parade"

*Courtesy of South High School Spectra*

As the parade snaked its way toward the Kent County Airport, the B-17 Flying Fortress bomber sat waiting, *The Spirit of South High, Grand Rapids, Michigan* clearly painted on both sides of the fuselage. It had arrived earlier from Lockbourne Army Air Force Base in Columbus, Ohio. Many reported watching it circle the city before landing.

On board were Colonel A. C. Foulk, base commander and a crew of eight, including Private Walter J. Fydrych, a Grand Rapids native stationed at the Lockbourne. Pvt. Fydrych who hadn't been home in two months surprised his wife at the ceremony. Colonel Foulk gave him overnight leave to spend time with his family.

The parade of students arrived at the airport to the applause of a crowd estimated to be over five thousand. As the band took its place under the left wing of the bomber, the Queen and her attendants, along with the bomber committee, mounted the stairs to the grandstand where military, state, county and city officials stood waiting.

Camp Fire girls unfurled a huge American flag.

State and local dignitaries took to the microphone to express their pride and admiration for what the students of South High School had accomplished. Brief remarks were made by Michigan Governor Harry F. Kelly, Colonel Edward C. Black, commanding officer of the Army Air Force technical training command, Mayor George Welsh, Henry B. Mulder, Harry Brown and Lieutenant Jack Goebel, a South High graduate and veteran of the North African campaign.

Queen LaVonne Kronberg, Col. A.C. Foulk, Mr. Henry Mulder, Mr. Harry Brown

In a solemn moment, Principal Sherman Coryell read the names of South High students, faculty and graduates who had lost their lives in the present conflict. A special section of the bleachers had been set aside for their Gold Star families.

Colonel A. C. Foulk praised the students and added, "Soon the United States Air Force will not rank with the best. They will be the best in the world!"

General Ralph Royce, commander of the Army Air Force through whose efforts the bomber was flown into Grand Rapids, could not attend. He sent the following telegram to Ruth Ann Jenkins, secretary of the school bond drive:

*Students and friends of South High school are to be congratulated upon the tremendous and worthwhile job that has been done in selling more than $375,000 worth of war bonds. The B-17 Flying Fortress that you are to dedicate today will serve as a symbol and an inspiration to our pilot and air crew members of this great ship that the people back home have not forgotten.*

*I am sure that with this inspiration they will go on and continue the great work that our air crews have been doing. I only regret that the press of my official duties prevents me from attending this ceremony personally, but my best wishes and hopes for your contributions toward our war effort are embodied in the Flying Fortress you see before you.*

*General Ralph Royce*
*Commander Army Air Force*

The crowd cheered as Queen Kronberg released six red and white balloons into the sky after christening the B-17 Flying Fortress, *The Spirit of South High.*[27]

Queen LaVonne Kronberg releases balloons at the christening ceremony of *The Spirit of South High.*

A crowd estimated well over five thousand watched the christening.

The parking lot was full.

Speakers included Governor H. Kelly, Mayor W. Welsh, Col. Foulk, Col. Black, commanding officer of AAF Technical Training Command, Mr. Mulder and Lt. Jack Goebel, South High graduate and veteran of the North African Campaign.

South High School's Band played.

Queen LaVonne Kronberg, Jean Endsley, Velma Kling, Lucille Hice, Barbara Northway, Margaret McCarthy with Col. Foulk.

44

The "Spirit of South High" roared down the runway and lifted into the air on the wings and prayers of fifteen hundred young students who believed that their bomber would emerge victorious in battles fought to turn the tide of the war toward victory and bring their fathers and brothers and uncles home.

Chapter Six
# The Pledges Keep Coming

"Bomber Day" was an event that would not soon be forgotten. Recognition for what South High students had accomplished drew national attention when a government magazine featured an article showing what can be achieved when a school sets a War Bond goal, along with a photograph of the christening of *The Spirit of South High*. Schools all over the United States received the magazine.

*The March 25, 1943 issue of the South High Tattler reported that Mr. Brown, Chairman of the Kent County Retailers' War Savings Committee, said he believed that South High School was the only school in the United States to have a bomber sent to its school to christen.*

Although the christening ceremony signaled the end to the "Buy a Bomber" campaign, War Bond purchases credited to South High continued to arrive. In addition, the sale of bonds and stamps within the school kept growing. The Student Council decided the time for a new campaign had arrived.

Through hard work and dedication, South High students had already placed two airplanes, one an advanced trainer plane and one a B-17 Flying Fortress bomber, in the air. Their next campaign focused on equipment to be designated for land; disaster vehicles described as combination canteens, ambulances and hospital cars. The goal of the new drive was to purchase one disaster vehicle a week at twenty-five hundred dollars each, until June 11th, the end of the school year. The first vehicle was to have a plaque posted inside indicating it was purchased by South High School. Additional vehicles were to each carry the name of an elementary school helping in the campaign. By the date of the christening of the bomber on April 6th, two disaster vehicles had already been purchased.[28]

The willingness of the administrators, faculty and students at South High to help in the war effort was highlighted in a different way when its amateur Radio Station WKHA, the largest of seventeen local amateur stations, was asked by the United States government to connect to the War Emergency Radio unit. This was an honor that held tremendous responsibility. Should an actual emergency occur and all other communications be destroyed, the responsibility to report fires, bombings, casualties, blocked roads, utility damages and other emergencies would fall to the school's radio station.[29]

As the academic year wound to a close, conversations throughout the school often turned toward *The Spirit of South High*. Students listened to radio broadcasts and watched newsreels at the movies straining to hear or see if any of the bombers mentioned bore the name of their flagship.

What about the bomber? Where was it now? How many battles had it won? How many Japanese or German planes had it destroyed? Speculation continued and rumors persisted that South High's bomber, their bomber, *The Spirit of South High*, was a major player in battles currently being fought and won.

## Chapter Seven
# School year 1943-1944

When school began in the fall of 1943, the war was still going strong, yet students returned to the routine of school with enthusiasm, embracing new teachers and classes, renewing friendships separated by summer recess, joining clubs and organizations and participating in sports activities.

Senior Student Council, the student governing body of the high school, maintained strong leadership as Dave Dutcher, who co-chaired the successful War Bond bomber campaign the year before, moved into the position of president.

The sale of War Loan Stamps was once again a normal part of every session room's morning ritual. In October, a third funding campaign encouraged by the Grand Rapids School System to sell War Loan Stamps, was quietly begun at South with little organized effort or commitment. A couple weeks later, the school system published a report ranking all participating schools. South High, the school that had sold enough War Bonds to purchase two planes and two disaster vehicles six months earlier, was ranked near the bottom below several elementary schools.

This was not to be tolerated.

The Senior Student Council took immediate action and appointed a committee. The goal of the new campaign was to win the right to fly the recently authorized Minute Man Flag. To accomplish that, ninety percent of the student body was required to commit to purchasing one war stamp or more each week. The campaign committee reasoned if South High was the first to buy a bomber through the sale of War Bonds and War Loan Stamps, they could easily get sufficient commitments to sell enough stamps to be the first in Grand Rapids to fly the Minute Man Flag.

The student body was introduced to the Minute Man Flag committee at assemblies held on October 26, and since the ten cent price of one stamp was within reach for most, the students rallied. Once again, in a very short period of time, school spirit prevailed and South High won the right to fly the Minute Man Flag.

Official word came through on November 12, 1943 in the form of a certificate along with authorization to order the flag.

*Courtesy of Roger Warren taken 2015*

When the flag arrived, it was raised on the flag pole under the Stars and Stripes at a ceremony attended by all students. The flag would fly daily as long as the school maintained ninety percent participation in the War Loan Stamp Drive.[30]

Seven months had passed since South students watched their B-17 bomber, *The Spirit of South High*, fly off to war following the christening ceremony. In all that time the only information as to its whereabouts came from rumor and speculation. The bomber became a topic for conversation and debate. Students, faculty, administrators and many community members wanted to know, what happened to the bomber?

By mid-January, 1944, with the Minute Man Flag waving under the Stars and Stripes on South High School's flag pole, Student Council was ready to launch its fourth War Bond Drive. Past drives launched planes in the air and disaster vehicles on land and this time the focus was on the sea. Margery Grooters, a junior, stepped forward as chairman of the campaign. The goal of the new fund drive was the purchase of a fleet of fully equipped landing barges.

"Get involved!" and "Do your part!" were slogans stressed both at an assembly and again during intermission at a basketball game where the campaign was announced. Taking up the challenge, two sophomores, Bob Spry and Roger Dutcher, solicited for pledges in their neighborhood. When the boys secured bond pledges of $2500 in a single night for the sophomore class, their success prompted the committee to foster inter-class competitions. From then on representatives in each session room calculated pledge totals for their particular class before turning those totals over to the bond committee chairman as had been done in the past. The class competition worked. Students actively engaged in the campaign.

The purchase of a fleet of fully equipped landing barges was a lofty goal. As with the bomber drive, many south end merchants and community organizations agreed to participate.

The Boosters' Association from Burton Heights Junior High, the feeder school to South High, helped formulate plans encouraging any school or organization in the south end of Grand Rapids to add landing barges they may purchase to South High's fleet. The publicity worked. Within one month, much like the "Buy a Bomber" campaign, the students of South High School, with the help of the Grand Rapids community, ended the campaign successfully. Enough War Bonds were sold to purchase sixty-three fully equipped landing barges and another christening ceremony had to be planned.[31]

On April 12, 1944, four barges were brought in by truck from the factory in Holland, Michigan where they were made and put on display at Garfield Park. Over eighteen hundred students and Grand Rapids citizens witnessed the christening as Barge Queen, Mary Ellen Johnson did the honors. The thirty-six foot barges provided an impressive backdrop for the festivities.

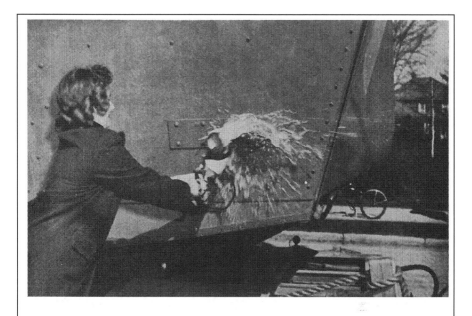

South High School's Barge Queen, Mary Ellen Johnson christens one of four barges in a fleet of sixty-three purchased through War Bond sales.

*Courtesy of 1944 South High School Spectra*

Representing the City of Grand Rapids, Mayor George W. Welsh said of South High, "The entire city is proud of what you have done, and if the country knew, it too, would be proud. Your example might well be followed by schools throughout the country."

Corporal Donald Derrick, a former South High student and veteran of landing campaigns in New Guinea, spoke of the value of the landing craft barges. "The barges are wonderful," he said. "With speed and power they take you from the transport to shore. The front drops down and you don't even get your feet wet."

Private Percy Jones, a veteran injured in New Guinea action said, "If we had had barges instead of rafts when we landed in New Guinea there might be a lot more men coming back."

The Chairman of the Navy Citizens Committee, Ted Booth, praised South High for its long record of achievement. Additional speakers included Horace H. Clark representing merchants who took part in the campaign, Henry B. Mulder, Faculty Advisor, Dave Dutcher, Student Council President and Barge Bond Chairman, Margery

Well over 1800 students, faculty, parents, community leaders and residents turned out to tour the landing barges and witness the christening.

*Courtesy of 1944 South High School Spectra*

Grooters. The ceremony concluded with a memorial ceremony for Gold Star alumni of South High school, led by the Captain of South's ROTC unit, Ward Thurston. [33]

*U.S. Army Signal Corps photograph, Gift in Memory of Maurice T. White, Collection of The National WWII Museum*

Contributions to the barge campaign affected pledges directed at the Minute Man Flag drive. By the end of April, several session rooms had fallen short, missing the 90% mark. The flag that had flown so proudly since November, 1943 had to be lowered. Nearly a month would pass before sales raised enough to fly the flag again.

On June 6, 1944, as Dave Dutcher, the young man who co-chaired the "Buy a Bomber" campaign in 1943 and actively participated in all the other bond drives, and his classmates prepared to graduate from their beloved South High school, one hundred fifty-six thousand soldiers stormed the beaches of Normandy, France. Dave and the young men graduating beside him that day knew what their future held. If they didn't enlist they would be drafted.

The war would rage on for another year and three months. In all that time and for years after, South High alums and interested community folks wondered where *The Spirit of South High* figured in. Did it distinguish itself? Was it victorious in battle? Did it keep its crew safe? What about the bomber?

## Chapter Eight
# The Bomber and the President

What happened to the bomber? That question has traveled through the decades. From students in the classes of 1943 through 1948 who participated in the "Buy a Bomber" campaign, to students in succeeding classes who heard about it, people wanted to know.

In 1968, when the doors of South High closed forever, the question still hadn't been answered. The closing, which occurred to comply with desegregation rulings and achieve racial balance in the other four Grand Rapids high schools, temporarily devastated the community, but it never crushed the spirit of those who had attended or graduated from South High School.[34]

That spirit rose again in 1990 when Robert Tuffelmire, a South High graduate who was a child during the bomber campaign, decided it was time to find the bomber.

A historian by trade, Tuffelmire began by searching old newspaper articles, historical archives and military offices. Personnel at the Army Air Force Historical Research Center in Mobile, Alabama were encouraging but indicated that the search might take some time. After months and months of waiting, Tuffelmire decided to try a different approach. He wrote to former President Gerald R. Ford.[35]

President Gerald R. Ford is one of the most famous of all South High graduates. It was at South High that he first ran for President, an election for president of the Class of 1931. Even though he lost that election to classmate Bill Schuili, his leadership skills were already evident. During his senior year he became an Eagle Scout and served as Captain of South High's winning football team. That year, over a Thanksgiving Day breakfast before a game with a rival school, the thirty members of the 1930 football team started a club they called, "The 30-30 Club." From that breakfast a tradition began that was to carry on well into the 1990's. The most notable of all the breakfasts occurred on Thanksgiving Day, 1974, when Gerald R. Ford, now President of the United States, welcomed the surviving members of "The 30-30 Club" to the White House.

Thanksgiving Day, 1974, President Ford with the 30-30 Club.
*Courtesy Gerald R. Ford Presidential Library.*

Thanksgiving Day, 1974, President Ford with the 30-30 Club.
*Courtesy Gerald R. Ford Presidential Library.*

President Ford's loyalty to his high school alma mater was well known among South High graduates. Naturally Tuffelmire thought of him when all other roads met dead ends. From his ranch in California where he had retired after leaving office in 1977, President Ford responded. He contacted Maxwell Air Force Base Historians and asked them to retrieve the files on *The Spirit of South High*.

Finally, the long awaited answer arrived, but it wasn't what Tuffelmire or any other South High graduate imagined. *The Spirit of South High*, hadn't won any battles. There were no notches on the fuselage for air strikes or kills. It hadn't lived the charmed wartime life some spoke of or met a brutal demise over the Pacific. It hadn't even been in a battle. The beloved B-17 Flying Fortress Bomber christened *The Spirit of South High* that legends had been

61

made of had been used for twenty-one months for pilot training and later dismantled.

The disappointing news spread quickly among former classmates. Like air exploding from a pricked balloon, the words in that letter deflated years of hopes and dreams and fables and legends. The once lost B-17 Flying Fortress bomber, purchased forty-eight years earlier when a group of junior high and senior high students accomplished the extraordinary by securing over $300,000 in War Bond pledges and winning the right to name it, *The Spirit of South High*, had finally had been found.

The story was over. Finished! The end!

Or was it?

# PART TWO

# *THE B-17 BOMBER*

## Chapter Nine
# Trouble in the Sky

Just after midnight on October, 1, 1944, a B-17 bomber taxied to the runway at Maxwell Army Air Force Base in Montgomery, Alabama. The pilot pushed the throttles forward, and the bomber lifted into the midnight sky. The bomber, serial number 42-29577 and christened eighteen months earlier as *The Spirit of South High,* was on the last leg of a short training mission, a quick turn-around flight. It had already transported an officer to Maxwell Field and was returning to Lockbourne Army Air Force Base in Columbus, Ohio. Estimated time of arrival (ETA) was 02:55.

On board were flight instructor Captain Arval Streadbeck, engineer Private First Class Ralph Poore, and four pilots training to become airplane Commanders, First Lieutenant Hearty Fitchko, First Lieutenant W. Michael Hobin, First Lieutenant Charles Hall and First Lieutenant William Grimson. Captain Streadbeck, the instructor, was a seasoned combat pilot with over one thousand hours experience flying B-17s out of North Africa into Southern Europe. The four pilots in-training were seasoned veterans recently returned from flying combat missions in the European theatre.

Future Commanders were expected to thoroughly understand and be able to perform all crew positions, so to comply with that step in the training process, the pilots traded positions during the mission. First Lieutenant Hobin, who along with 1st Lt. Fitchko had been navigators on the way to Alabama, was in the co-pilot seat and 1st Lt. Fitchko was in the radio room. The navigators were now 1st Lt. Grimson and 1st Lt. Hall. Midway through the flight, 1st Lt. Fitchko and 1st Lt. Hobin would exchange places with 1st Lt. Fitchko becoming copilot and 1st Lt.Hobin assuming radio duties.

The Commanders-in-training also had to prove their night flying competence which is very different from flying during the day because they had to depend more on cockpit instruments and a different part of the eye is used. Unless lights were grouped, as when a town arranges their lights in a recognizable pattern like a runway, visual references diminish and the horizon is no longer obvious.[36] The flight to and from Lockbourne Army Air Force Base was a night mission and required pilots to rely on their instruments.

The pilots were also training to use the Norden Bombsight, a new piece of advanced technology that no other country had, an analog computer that allowed for accurate bombing during the war.[37]

On the ground at Maxwell all pre-flight systems checked out properly. Fuel levels were at eleven hundred gallons, and since the bomber had consumed six hundred gallons on the way to Maxwell Field, Capt. Streadbeck concluded that refueling was unnecessary. The supply was more than adequate for the three hour return flight to Lockbourne. Clearance was granted for takeoff.

Overcast conditions through which they had flown on their way to Maxwell Field persisted, but weather reports from Lockbourne, where they were now headed, indicated "light smoke and light fog." In the event visibility around the base in Ohio worsened, clearance was also given through to Buffalo, New York, as an alternate.

Maxwell field disappeared quickly as the bomber rose into the night sky heading back to Ohio.

Shortly after takeoff Capt. Streadbeck ordered Engineer Poore to transfer fuel from the left bomb bay tank—one of two reserve units in the B-17—into tank number four. The fuel log, recorded on the way to Maxwell Field, indicated the left bomb bay tank contained fifty gallons while the right bomb bay measured the full four hundred ten gallons. Engineer Poore started the transfer but after three minutes he noticed the gauge didn't change. He then switched to the right bomb bay tank with the same result. The fuel did not transfer.[38] Had it done so there would have been two additional hours of flying time available. Capt. Streadbeck throttled the engines back to seventeen hundred RPM to save fuel.

As the bomber headed north, the heavy undercover thickened. The plane was now flying through thick cloud formations at its assigned altitude of seven thousand feet;

above, rain clouds with thunder and lightning almost obscured the sky. The last visual fix was of a small town east of Chattanooga, Tennessee, which indicated the bomber was slightly off course. First Lieutenant Hobin and Capt. Streadbeck adjusted their heading by twenty-five degrees.

First Lieutenant Hall and 1st Lt. Grimson struggled for accurate readings from the radio compass and the radio directional finder yet both instruments were adversely affected by the weather. The magnetic compass had been fluctuating erratically sixty to one hundred twenty degrees from side to side, rendering it useless. Radio beams broadcast from antennas on the ground were building, getting louder, and fading and disappearing all together, making it impossible for the pilots to know for sure what range or quadrant they were coming from. As soon as one was identified it would fade away before a beam crossing could be established. At one point signals were coming in from opposite sides of the course with similar strength, so the pilots believed the course they were flying was nearly true. On three other occasions, quadrant signals of several beams provided a very rough fix on their position.[39]

Captain Streadbeck made calls to Columbus radio with both the Command and Liaison transmitters but the Liaison transmitter was out of commission. He also made calls to Lockbourne with no response. [40]

When the bomber flew through what the crew thought was the southeast leg of the Cincinnati range, the navigators were finally able to tune in the Columbus range.

The beam came in strong. But ten minutes before their ETA of 02:55, that connection also died out. First Lieutenant Fitchko and Capt. Streadbeck worked frantically to reestablish the Columbus beam, but didn't succeed. Capt. Streadbeck once again made several attempts to reach Lockbourne by radio without success.[41]

Thirty minutes past their ETA, 1st Lt. Hall and 1st Lt. Grimson verified a slight build on the signal from the Cleveland Range and since Cleveland was not far off from Buffalo, the alternate landing location, they turned the plane accordingly. Gas gauges at the time indicated six hundred gallons of fuel; however, one of the gauges had stuck at three quarters.[42] Engineer Poore estimated the tanks at five hundred gallons or a little more than two hours flying time remaining.

The bomber flew on as the crew worked feverishly to establish their position. At 04:15, an hour and fifteen minutes beyond ETA, Fitchko thought he saw the lights of a landing strip through a small break in the clouds. Capt. Streadbeck descended the plane to three thousand feet but found only a tiny town with street lamps paralleling a road. The bomber climbed back up to seven thousand feet, above the cloud layers.[43]

> "...there was no airport open between the Mississippi and the Atlantic. All we could do was fly around until our gas ran out."
>
> *Captain Arval Streadbeck*

Captain Streadbeck would later write: *"The Columbus range now came in loud and clear. We turned to 320 degrees, the N-bisector heading, and established a definite fade on the command set...The fade indicated that we should make a 180 degree turn for approximately fifteen minutes. It was now 04:30 and No. 2, 3 and 4 tanks were indicating practically empty. No. 1 tank still indicated ¾ full. About this time the station began to fade, and the No. 4 engine ran out of gas. I tried to feather the engine but it would not stay in the feathered position.[44] The RPM on No. 4 went up to 2700 and No. 1 engine ran out of gas. I ordered all four of the men to the rear of the plane to stand by for bail out."[45]*

The plane was still at seven thousand feet but with two engines out, it began to circle.

Private First Class Poore set parachutes behind Capt. Streadbeck's and 1st Lt. Fitchko's seats and went back to the waist, in the middle of the plane, and kicked open the escape door. First Lieutenant Grimson, 1st Lt. Hobin and 1st Lt. Hall, along with Pfc. Poore, strapped their parachutes in place and waited for the signal to jump, a long drawn-out bell. All were silent. There was no panic. There was no time. They'd done what they had been trained to do--follow orders.[46] When the bell rang, one of the men in the waist merely said, "There it is!"[47]

Private First Class Poore jumped first followed by 1st Lt. Hobin, then 1st Lt. Grimson and 1st Lt. Hall. First Lieutenant Fitchko released the escape hatch in the nose and waited with Capt. Streadbeck. About five minutes later the number three engine began to sputter. The plane was losing altitude. The Captain ordered 1st Lt. Fitchko to bail.

Now alone in the cockpit, Capt. Streadbeck watched the controls as the bomber *"circled out of a cloud into the open above the overcast, descending to 6,000 feet. I noticed that I had made a complete 360 degree circle and the heading was 120 degrees. I trimmed the ship for straight and level flight and the third engine, No. 3, ran out of gas. I went down to the radio hatch and jumped. As I fell back downward, I saw the ship [plane] well above."*[48]

# Chapter Ten
# Bailing Out

Private First Class Poore was shaken but conscious when his oversized parachute opened, the straps badly burning his chest and inner thighs.[49] He could see the bomber disappearing in the distance as he floated into the thick fog. Landing hard on the side of a sparsely wooded hill, he badly bruised his back and shoulder although he wouldn't realize it until later. He gathered up his parachute and walked in the direction the plane had taken, hollering out for his other crew members.

First Lieutenant Hobin had tumbled out of the plane spinning over and over. Training taught him to raise his head and straighten his body to stop the rotation. It worked. He lowered his head and spun a second time. By the time his parachute opened, he was well into the dense fog. Then he hit the ground. He never saw it coming or had time to prepare for landing. He felt his leg snap and knew the break was bad.[50]

First Lieutenant Grimson had jumped next and was soon engulfed in the dense fog that extended all the way to the ground. Small trees sticking through were the only indication that the ground was near. As soon as he hit the ground he heard 1st Lt. Hobin's screams for help. A few minutes later he located him.

First Lieutenant Hall had bailed next, landing a short distance away from 1st Lt. Grimson and 1st Lt. Hobin.

After climbing three hills and shouting for the others as he went, Pfc. Poore finally heard someone holler back. Shortly thereafter, he found 1st Lt. Grimson and 1st Lt. Hall. They were huddled over 1st Lt. Hobin.

Although all of the men were injured, their focus was on 1st Lt. Hobin who was going into shock. One of them had to go for help and 1st Lt. Grimson was elected. He tried to get his bearings in the foggy surroundings as he limped away into the mist. For over an hour and a half he walked until he found a farmhouse where he could call for help.

First Lieutenant Fitchko bailed out of the escape hatch in the nose, feet first, and tumbled three or four somersaults before pulling the rip cord. His parachute opened when he was upside down, violently jerking him upward. He looked up as the plane passed overhead, close to him, the last engine blasting fire. Through the haze a few seconds later, he saw the plane hit and burst into flames. By his own account he "... *landed quite hard in an open spot, near a wooded area about three-quarters of a mile from the crash. After getting out of the harness, I bundled up the chute and tried to pick up my bearings. I called for Capt. Streadbeck but no one answered. I walked over a hill and down in the valley. I stumbled into a house but it was deserted. Luckily, a car drove by about five hundred feet away* so I headed for the road. The brush and briars were pretty thick but I managed to get up to the road. Once on the road, I followed it in the direction of the crash. Over the road and about five hundred feet from the crash, I saw a house with some lights so I took my parachute over."[51]

Captain Streadbeck left the ship falling backward looking up as the bomber flew by overhead. "I pulled the rip cord and tensed myself for the big jerk of the opening chute but it never came. The chute opened slowly and evenly and my only sensation was that of being on a big swing.

The ship continued on course for several hundred feet and then gradually made a turn to the left. As it turned it descended, making a complete 360 degree turn before it disappeared into the overcast. I saw a bright flash of fire about a mile away from me and soon later [heard] an explosion.

As I swung pleasantly to and fro, I passed through layer after layer of clouds and rain. Then I saw pine tree tops rush past and I landed with a thud and splash in the mud on the side of a mountain. My right foot pained me and I was out of breath. After lying there for a few minutes I tried to move. First I moved my arms. They seemed to be all right so I looked at my watch. It was five o'clock in the morning. Next I moved my legs and finally tried to get up. Everything seemed all right. [Looking up,] I thought I could see the top of the mountain nearby. If I could get there, I could probably see where the plane had crashed. I didn't want to leave my parachute so I gathered it up in my arms and started climbing. Two or three fences later I was at the top and could see lights of a farm house in the canyon below me on the other side. I hollered."[52]

# PART THREE

# *THE BLUE RIDGE*

# *PARKWAY*

Mile Marker 176.2 – The Blue Ridge Parkway

*Taken by Sandra Warren, 2015*

## Chapter Eleven
# Rescued

"Momma! Momma! Wake up! A plane crashed! It did momma!" Six year old Aaron McAlexander ran into his mother's bedroom.

"You're dreaming again," his sleepy mother said.

"No I'm not!" Aaron insisted. "The whole house shook! Didn't you feel it? A plane crashed! I know it did."

"Aaron, if a plane crashed I certainly would have heard it as would your sister and she's still fast asleep. Now go back to bed!" Exhausted from taking care of the family and the farm while her husband was fighting overseas, Aaron's mother was not to be swayed. He stomped back to his bedroom and stared out the window.[53]

A few miles away, eight year old Arlie Dalton heard it too. The sound of a screaming engine woke him up. The noise grew louder and louder, but by the time Arlie got to the window, the noise had stopped. A few seconds later he saw a huge ball of fire shoot several hundred feet into the air and rise over the tree tops. The fire appeared to come from his grandpa's farm but he was unsure because there was a hill in the way.[54]

Mary Edith Goad was nineteen when the plane roared overhead, just missed her parents' farmhouse and clipped some pine trees before crashing. "It was the sound of the plane that woke us and by the time we got up it had crashed. The whole house shook," Mary said. "I thought the plane was coming right at us."[55]

First Lieutenant Fitchko had been walking for quite a while in the dark rainy mist before spotting lights in a farmhouse. The lady who answered his knock identified herself as a Mrs. Goad. When 1st Lt. Fitchko asked Mrs. Goad where he was, she said, "In Meadows of Dan."

"Where's that?" he asked.

"Virginia," Mrs. Goad said.

"Oh my God! We thought we were in Ohio," 1st Lt. Fitchko said.[56] Meadows of Dan, Virginia, was over two hundred fifty miles from their Ohio destination.

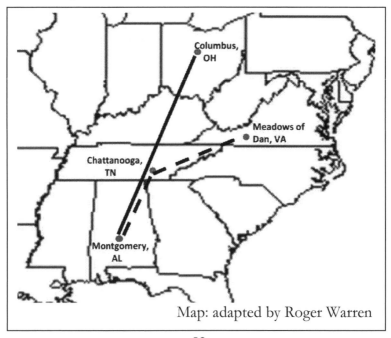

Map: adapted by Roger Warren

When asked if she had a telephone he could use, Mrs. Goad said no, but she was sure one of the men at the crash might be able to drive him to one. "My husband's over by the plane...took the kerosene lantern with him." She pointed to a spot about five hundred feet from the house.

First Lieutenant Fitchko then asked permission to leave his parachute on her porch telling her that a salvage crew would be by to pick it up later. She agreed and directed him toward the scene.

First Lieutenant Fitchko was the first of the pilots to arrive at the crash site. Most of the fire had died down and people were probing around for victims. First Lieutenant Fitchko told them that although he couldn't verify the whereabouts of the crew, he was fairly confident they had all gotten out safely.

When 1st Lt. Fitchko asked if anyone had a telephone he could use, Mr. D. L. Handy offered to drive him to the nearest switchboard and wait while he placed the call to his base. By this time, over an hour had passed since the plane had come down. When the operator placed the call, she asked 1st Lt. Fitchko if he was the same fellow who called Lockbourne Army Air Base a short while before. It was from her that 1st Lt. Fitchko learned that another crew member had survived.

After the call, Mr. Handy took 1st Lt. Fitchko back to his house and gave him some much needed coffee.[57]

The sound of the bomber circling overhead, followed by the thunder of the crash, was what woke the Barnard family. By the time thirteen-year-old Vera hurried

83

downstairs, her father had the front door open and was looking out. He shushed Vera and her two sisters as he cocked his head toward the mountain, listening.

He heard a call for help in the distance. Vera's father shouted back and then disappeared into the dark foggy morning. He returned to the house several minutes later helping a military man who was clutching a parachute. The man had bailed out of his aircraft and had hurt his foot upon landing. He identified himself as United States Army Air Force Capt. Arval Streadbeck.

The Captain limped through the door and handed Vera's sister, Jesse, the parachute. "Keep this and make your wedding dress out of it," he jokingly said.[58]

Jesse clutched the parachute to her chest and swooned.

Although injured, the very nervous Capt. Streadbeck expressed concern for his crew who he had ordered to bail after three of the four engines ran out of fuel and quit. He asked if Vera's father had heard any other calls for help. The reply was "No."

Captain Streadbeck continued talking. His parachute had just opened when the plane circled around and narrowly missed him. He wasn't sure what his fate would be for losing a B-17 bomber.

Shaking, the Captain asked if there was a telephone he could use. Lockbourne Army Air Force Base had to be notified and the crash reported to his superior officer. Vera's mother showed him the old telephone hanging on the wall. He cranked the handle and waited for an operator.

By this time, the telephone operator at the exchange that early morning was busy dealing with multiple persons chattering about the crash. With some difficulty, she cleared the lines so Capt. Streadbeck could get a call through to his commanding officer. His message needed to be routed by a number of operators, through various telephone exchanges, each, in turn, requiring lines to be cleared to get a long distance call through to Ohio. The process was time consuming and especially stressful for the injured captain since at the time of the call, Capt. Streadbeck did not know the fate of the other members of his crew, if they were injured, or if they had even survived.

Captain Streadbeck talked to the telephone operator while waiting for his call to connect. Through the operator he learned of the location of the crash. After reporting to his commanding officer, he asked Vera's father if he could be taken to where the plane had come down. Mr. Barnard bundled his family along with Capt. Streadbeck into his car and drove them to the crash site. Once there they all stood staring in disbelief.

The bomber had crashed in farmer Charlie "Bud" Goad's pig lot, just missing the family house and historic Mabry's Mill on the Blue Ridge Parkway. The wreckage scattered debris over two hundred yards.

> "The debris went into a pig lot but it didn't kill or injure a single pig!"
>
> *Ruth Jean Bolt*

Three of the four engines were buried in the swamp. This B-17 bomber, measuring approximately seventy feet from nose to tail and one hundred four feet wing tip to wing tip, was a pile of rubble.

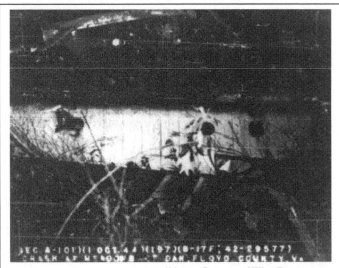

*Photos Courtesy of War Department*
*U.S. Army Air Forces Report of Accident*
*Mike Stowe Accident-report.com*

State Police Officer H.C. Birkhead from Stuart, Virginia, was the first local man of authority to arrive at the scene. "I immediately deputized him [officer Birkhead] to take charge of the wreckage and to deputize others to secure the site until Army Guards could arrive," Capt. Streadbeck said.[59] "Of prime concern were such things as the Norden Bombsight, the new technology that allowed for accurate bombing. I had to make sure all the military equipment was protected."[60]

That accomplished, the Captain, now limping badly, was taken to the Goad farmhouse so he could sit down for treatment. There at the Goad house he learned 1st Lt. Fitchko was safe and at a nearby farm. Shortly thereafter Mr. Handy brought 1st Lt. Fitchko to the Goads' where several neighbors had gathered around Capt. Streadbeck with concern for his injured foot. From these people the pilots learned there was a military hospital in Roanoke, Virginia, about sixty miles away. Getting there would prove challenging. Gas rationing limited the use of local vehicles. After much discussion, Mr. Walter Cochran offered to drive the pilots to the bus station in the nearby town of Floyd where they could catch a bus to Roanoke.

Meanwhile, on the side of a mountain, an injured 1st Lt. Grimson trudged forward for over an hour and a half searching for help knowing his three other crew members were depending on him. By the time he located a farmhouse with lights on, it was already 06:30. The farmer and his wife took him inside and listened while he told of the other three men. They had heard about the plane crash over in Meadows of Dan, about fourteen miles away, and were surprised to see a crew member at their door.

The farmer called for the local doctor and an ambulance. While they waited, Grimson called Lockbourne and was connected to the Officer of the Day.

A short while later a hearse, doubling as an ambulance, arrived with the doctor inside. Painted on its side was the company name, Mayberry Funeral Home. The doctor noted that Grimson was spitting blood and ordered him to lie down while they went for the other crew members. The farmer assured Grimson that together he, the doctor and the ambulance driver could find the others and come back for him.

Not until the crew was in the ambulance did they learn they were in Willis, Virginia, two-hundred and fifty miles off course.

First Lieutenant Hall was sitting in the front seat of the ambulance as it traveled through Floyd, Virginia on its way to the Veteran's Hospital in Roanoke, when he noticed Capt. Streadbeck and 1st Lt. Fitchko struggling to stand at a street corner under a bus sign. First Lieutenant Fitchko spotted 1st Lt. Hall at the same time. The ambulance driver collected the other two and drove them all to the Roanoke hospital.

At the hospital, Capt. Streadbeck, 1st Lt. Fitchko and 1st Lt. Grimson were treated and released after talking to the military accident board officials. First Lieutenant Hall, 1st Lt. Hobin and Pfc. Poore were admitted.

First Lieutenant Hall sustained leg, foot and chest injuries. First Lieutenant Hobin broke his fibula, tibia and his ankle when his right leg took the brunt of the impact in the landing. His injuries would keep him in the hospital for eighty-three days. Private First Class Poore, with a severely bruised back and shoulder injuries as well as the burns from his parachute straps on his chest and inner thighs, remained in the hospital when 1st Lt. Hobin was released.[61]

## Chapter Twelve
# The Clean-Up

Sunday afternoon, just hours after the crash, Major Freck of the Office of Flying Safety in Winston-Salem, North Carolina, arrived to conduct an investigation.[62] Four days later a group of civil service employees from the Charlotte, North Carolina Air Base brought in equipment to salvage the wreckage.[63]

"Six to eight men came to do the work with four flatbed trucks; one truck had a crane on it and winches to lift the largest pieces," Arlie Dalton remembers. He lived with his grandparents on the property where the plane came down. "There were no motels in the area at the time so the men bunked in my grandfather's barn. I'm not sure who fed them but I'm guessing it was my grandma."[64]

With debris scattered over approximately two hundred yards of Mr. Goad's farm, the salvage process was enormous. The engines presented the biggest challenge. Three of them were buried deep in the muddy swamp and a fourth was missing.

*Courtesy of War Department*
*U.S. Army Air Forces Report of Accident*
*Mike Stowe Accident-report.com*

The crew managed to retrieve the three and were hunting for the fourth engine when a man, Nick Bowman, a wandering handy-man, emerged from the woods wearing an Army cap he'd just found. When Nick learned what the salvage crew was looking for, he pointed and said, "It's over there behind that log thicket." To show their gratitude for finding the engine, the crew told Nick to keep the hat for a souvenir.[65]

Arlie also noted that "After the salvage crew hauled four or five [round-trip] loads of the largest pieces of scrap metal from the property, the foreman came to my Grandpa and asked him if it was clean enough? When Grandpa said, 'yep!' he asked Grandpa to sign a paper stating that it was okay to leave the small scrap. The foreman said he didn't want to haul it off. Grandpa didn't mind. He was a handyman and carpenter. He liked to make stuff."[66]

Before the crash site was secured and after the wrecking crews left, scores of town folk visited the site and picked up souvenirs. Parts of wings, propellers, scrap fittings from the control board, nuts and bolts were among the treasured items. Arlie Burnette, and Alfred and Dot Cruise, all children at the time, remember the kids picking up small pieces of scrap and fashioning rings out of them.[67] [68] Even Grandpa Goad was known to have created a ring or two. [69] Six-year-old Aaron McAlexander found an aircraft fuel filter and has been using it as a paperweight for the last seventy-one years.[70]

## Chapter Thirteen
# A Different Perspective

In 1991, when Robert Tuffelmire received the news from the Maxwell Air Force Base Historians that *The Spirit of South High*, the B-17 Flying Fortress bomber that the students had put their hearts and souls into, was used for training and never saw combat, there was great disappointment. "Truffelmire said many of his former classmates were disheartened to learn the aircraft had not seen combat..." and "The students of South High feel they've been cheated because our hearts were really into it," are two of the quotes published in an article in the *Grand Rapids Press* about the discovery. [71]

Seventy-two years later a different perspective is offered.

The bomber christened *The Spirit of South High* may not have experienced combat first hand but that does not mean it wasn't front and center in some of the most difficult and most heroic battles of the war.

How?

*The Spirit of South High* was used to train pilots and crew; navigators, bombardiers, radio operators, engineers and gunners. The average B-17 crew consisted of ten men. And although each training mission may not have included all ten, multiple missions flown over the twenty-one months the bomber was in commission would have trained upwards of two-thousand men.

Three of the men serving on the last mission of *The Spirit of South High,* that fateful day in October of 1944, had exemplary military records:

1st Lt. W. Michael Hobin is second from the left. The other crew members in the photo in front of a B-25 were not assigned to *The Spirit of South High.*

*Courtesy of Major W. Michael Hobin*

First Lieutenant W. Michael Hobin returned to the United States to take Commander Instructor Pilot Training after flying a B-17 Flying Fortress bomber in twenty-six combat missions over Germany. Following Instructor Pilot

Training, he assumed transportation duty in Michigan flying B-24 aircraft from production in Michigan to Oklahoma for armament. He later transferred to Florida for training on C-54s and eventually flew C-54s into Tokyo and brought out Dutch prisoners of war. While in the military, 1st Lt. Michael Hobin achieved the rank of Major and served in the Army Air Force for eighteen more years.[72]

First Lieutenant Fitchko, who was twenty-two years old when he served as co-pilot on *The Spirit of South High's* last day, became a well-known WWII "Ace." He flew twenty-nine bombing missions from England in a B-17 and was one of the youngest squadron leaders ever in the United States Air Force. During bombing missions he parachuted to safety twice, qualifying him for membership in the honored Caterpillar Club. He was instrumental in developing the delivery method used to drop the A-Bomb on Hiroshima while serving with the 509th Parachute Infantry Regimen. After WWII, Colonel Fitchko set a world air speed record by flying a B-58 coast to coast. He was then inducted into the Strategic Air Command and piloted B-47's and B52's. He retired a highly decorated Colonel in 1966. Col. Fitchko was awarded the Distinguished Flying Cross among several prestigious medals and honors."[73]

Captain Arval L. Streadbeck, the flight instructor, was in the 2nd Bomb Group involved in the Air Offensive Europe campaign, flying fifty-two combat missions, and attaining 50 qualified sorties out of North Africa into

Southern Europe. In North Africa he piloted B-17 aircraft. Prior to arriving in North Africa, he had also qualified in B-24 aircraft, and following the attainment of his 50 combat sorties, he returned to the States where he trained pilots in B-17s and later in B-29s. He achieved the rank of Major.[74]

Captain Arval Streadbeck is in the second row wearing the helmet. He's pictured with his B-17, named Sad Sack, and crew in Africa. Bomber was named after a comic strip popular at the time.

*Courtesy of Major Arval Streadbeck*

Major Arval L. Streadbeck, his wife Julia and son Larry.
*Courtesy of Major Arval Streadbeck*

Captain Streadbeck was inducted into the honored Caterpillar Club after the surviving the bail out on October 1, 1944.

The outstanding records of these three military men are but a tiny sample of the quality of the men who trained on *The Spirit of South High*. The members of the class of 1943 and all those who worked tirelessly to purchase the bomber, have no reason to be disheartened any longer.

*The Spirit of South High* lived no charmed wartime life as many had hoped or suffered no brutal demise over the Pacific Ocean as some had speculated. It did much, much more. It prepared thousands of young men to fly the B-17 Flying Fortress Bomber, the plane the Germans called the dreaded "four-motors,"[75] in every theatre of the war and through the most difficult conditions.

Be proud students of South High, especially the Class of 1943. What you did was extraordinary!

You bought a B-17 Flying Fortress Training Bomber!

# Tying Up Loose Ends

**The Fighter/War Plane:**

In all the excitement about raising $300,000 to purchase the B-17 bomber, the first successful War Bond campaign to purchase the fighter plane was all but forgotten. That campaign raised $75,000. And to answer a question that many have, "Yes," there really was a plane.[76] However, the AT-6A plane was not a fighter plane. It was an advanced trainer and never used in combat. In addition, I could find no indication there was a dedication ceremony.

Queen LaVonne Kronberg, Jean Endsley, Velma Kling, Lucille Hice, Barbara Northway, Margaret McCarthy AT-6A Advanced Trainer

The plane was an AT-6A North American Texan Trainer, Serial number 115903, a two-seater, the preferred plane used to train United States military pilots because it had many of the same features of the larger, more sophisticated fighters, bombers and transport planes.[77] Most of the planes involved in the War Bond "Buy a Bomber" program were trainers.[78]

The trainer aircraft number 41-15903 was built in 1941 and is believed to have been used as a trainer from that time forth. By February, 1943, when it was purchased by students in South High's first "Buy a Bomber" funding drive, it had trained many fighter pilots.

In the fall of 1944, South's Texan Trainer experienced the same fate as South's B-17; it crashed and was later scrapped. The pilot, Second Lieutenant James A. Plaunt had made a routine three-point landing and had requested permission to make a cross-wind take-off from a different runway at Chanute Field in Illinois. The control tower granted him permission at his own discretion. On take-off the plane ground looped[79] to the right, collapsing the left gear and causing major damage to the left wing.[80]

This plane was the first to be named, *The Spirit of South High*, although the title does not appear to be painted on its side. Ironically, even though the Texas Trainer had survived three other crashes, the final accident for the Texan Trainer occurred on September 27, 1944, three days before the B-17 *Spirit of South High,* ran out of fuel over Meadows of Dan, Virginia.

Aircraft 41-15903 -AT-6A – Crash, Chanute Field, Illinois.
*Courtesy of War Department U.S. Army Air Forces Report of Accident*
*Mike Stowe Accident-report.com*

## Bomber: Serial # 42-29577, *The Spirit of South High:*

Where did the number forty-two (42) come from when the number on the tail is clearly a thirty-two (32)? The forty-two refers to the year the bomber was made. The first number of that year (in this case a four) is often left off of communications. The large 32 on the tail referenced the squadron number or sometimes the aircraft Bureau number.

Tail of "The Spirit of South High."

## Funding the B-17:

While researching this story I was continually frustrated by the fluctuating price tag on the B-17 bomber. In 1943, the Treasury Department listed the cost at $300,000 and that was the goal of the "Buy a Bomber" campaign. However, another report listed the cost as $240,000 and a third as $275,000. An account following 'Bomber Day' at the Kent County airport published in the book, *Grand Rapids Goes to War: The 1940's Homefront*, stated..."Recent investigation indicates the plane cost $340,000 to build."

104

But earlier that same article stated..."On April 2, 1943, with the $375,000 goal met, a B-17, The Spirit of South High, was flown to the Kent County Airport for its christening on April 6."[81]

What I do know for sure is that well over $375,000 was raised and a B-17 plus two disaster vehicles were funded. As fund raisers go, it was still an extraordinary accomplishment.

## War Fund Drive: The "Buy a Bomber" Campaign:

South High School was not alone in its purchase of a bomber. Many other cities, townships, businesses, societies and even schools became involved; everyone wanted to do their part. This was an exciting way to sell War Bonds and War Loan Stamps. The school was one of two hundred twenty known to have participated. (See APPENDIX).

South High's experience with the bomber ceremony appears to have been an exception. According to Ray Bowden of the USAAF Nose Art Research Project, early on, when a bomber was purchased, *"...the aircraft was flown to a local airfield and a naming ceremony was carried out with full publicity but, as the pressures of the war increased, this became impossible so the aircraft was painted up as it left the factory or modification facility and a photograph was sent to the community representatives or local newspapers."[82]*

*"...Research carried out by John Fredrickson [indicated that] some war bond aircraft never actually existed at all. He wrote 'At North American of Kansas, the ruse was carried out in the photographic department. A master photo of a generic B-25 was prepared...[with]*

*no serial number or other identifying marks. A calligrapher then inked the name of the contributing group onto paper. The image was photographed so the small cursive was then overlaid onto the generic negative. The actual 8 X 10 photo implied that there was an actual B-25 with white paint decorating the nose in celebration of their monetary contribution. Every group received a photo of the same airplane and nobody at the factory bothered to dab a brush into paint."*[83]

As bad as this seems, we must keep in mind that this was war time and the United States was building bombers at a rapid rate. "During 1942 – 1943, 185,000 war planes will be built. [A chart indicates] 60,000 (45,000 combat) in 1942 and 125,000 (100,000 combat) in 1943."[84] It wasn't that the money collected for War Bonds was improperly used, but rather, the promise proposed in the "Buy a Bomber" campaign wasn't kept. Even though the money did help pay for the production of military equipment, most likely the donors thought they were funding actual bombers. These deceptive tactics, had they been known at the time, would have served to deflate the enthusiasm surrounding the entire funding campaign.

## Recognizing *The Spirit of South High:*

Since B-17 bomber number 42-29577 was used as a training plane on United States soil, it is doubtful that the words *The Spirit of South High* remained painted on its fuselage. The military had strict policy about personalizing equipment while on home soil. Overseas pilots were allowed to creatively name their bombers. Research indicates that most of the names given to the "Buy a Bomber" aircraft were painted over. The crash damage to *The Spirit of South High* made it impossible to see if the words were still there.

## Captain Arval Streadbeck:

Some may question the events leading up to the demise of *The Spirit of South High,* but the weather was a major factor. Capt. Streadbeck learned later that seven other military aircraft crashed that same early morning, due to the heavy overcast conditions that blanketed the entire eastern United States. The other seven aircraft tried to land. They all crashed with no survivors. Only the crew of *The Spirit of South High* survived, because Capt. Streadbeck ordered them to bail.

## The Crash Site: Meadows of Dan, Virginia:

The *Spirit of South High* ended its final mission in a farmer's field and pig lot adjacent to one of the most photographed spots on the Blue Ridge Parkway, historic Mabry's Mill. At the time, Mabry's Mill had been under restoration by the National Parks System but work had been halted because funds were reassigned to the war effort. Acreage that included the crash site was sold to the National Park System shortly after the war.

*Courtesy, National Park Service, Blue Ridge Parkway*

The historic site is composed of a number of historic structures including the gristmill, sawmill and blacksmith shop where visitors can experience demonstrations and cultural exhibits depicting life in rural Virginia. In 1954, just a few hundred feet from where the bomber came down, a coffee shop was added and later expanded into a restaurant and gift shop. Leslie Shelor, a life-long resident in the area said that whenever her family ate at the restaurant her father would point out the window and say, "That's where the bomber crashed and an engine is still buried in the swamp."[85]

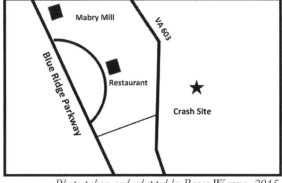

*Photo taken and adapted by Roger Warren, 2015*

On May 3, 2015, I had the pleasure of visiting the crash site along with two gentlemen who were children at the time of the crash, Arlie Burnette, and Arlie Dalton, grandson to Mr. Goad who had owned the farm and pig lot. As we stood there looking at the forest of trees, I asked Arlie Dalton if the pig lot looked different in 1943? He said, "Not a lot of difference. It is probably similar before the airplane crash as it is now, probably most of the trees on the edge have grown over the years but what's inside, scrubby trees and swamp, is pretty much the same."[86]

## Virginia: The People Remember

If Virginia is a place for lovers, as the motto says, then the cities of Meadows of Dan and Willis and Floyd are places of loving people. On that day in October, 1944 they embraced six scared and injured young men, and did what they could to help, no matter the hardship to themselves or their families.

In 1943, Meadows of Dan and the surrounding towns were small farming communities nestled in the Blue Ridge Mountains near the North Carolina line. People there lived a subsistence life-style, some barely able to feed their families. Many houses were without indoor plumbing and electricity and few had telephones. But the people were rich in culture, faith, family, music and love of country. And, like Americans throughout the United States, the people were sacrificing for the war effort.

Most of the men aged eighteen to thirty-eight were overseas in distant lands fighting. "...all of the younger men were gone, a lot of them...," shared Marie Terry Bowman. "In fact, my dad went into the service at age thirty-seven. He left a wife and seven children. He was drafted. Yes, Mom was home with seven children ages eleven and under!"[87]

When gas was rationed, the folks that had cars used them sparingly. Neighbors would double up and offer rides to each other. Aaron McAlexander reports being in his aunt's car and following a pickup truck, the bed filled with people sitting in straight-backed chairs headed toward the crash site. This was not unusual. Pick-up trucks were often used in this manner.[88]

Telephone service, especially long-distance, was very expensive, but Mr. Barnard didn't hesitate when Capt. Streadbeck asked to make a call, nor did Mr. Handy when 1st. Lt. Fitchko requested the same. When asked if it were true that her father never received reimbursement for that call, Vera Barnard Seigler said, "My father would never have asked for money from a service man. He never would have done that."[89]

The locals came forward and helped where they could.

For the next several days curiosity seekers came from far and near to see where the big bomber had crash landed. Many heard the rumble as the bomber circled the area and some felt the ground shake as it hit and exploded.

Six year old Aaron McAlexander reported being disappointed when he finally saw the site. "There were no pillars of smoke or roiling blazes, no craters in the earth and no path blasted through shattered trees. There were just a lot of big pieces of shiny metal scattered all over the field."[90]

Eleven-year old Patsy Cockram remembered her momma driving her to see the crash site. "...We lived eight to ten miles from Mabry Mill. Momma knew about it, got interested and took us there and we walked around the site...My step-brother was on a Flying Fortress [B-17] and he was captured by the Germans. They shot it down over Antwerp, Belgium...I guess that's one reason she went up there [to the crash site]."[91]

Marie Terry Bowman was eleven years old at the time and what she remembers the most about visiting the crash site were the pigs. "There was an old sow and a bunch of little piglets and it didn't kill any of them," she remembered. "It didn't destroy the fence around the pig lot either because...the pigs were still playing around the plane."[92]

Although the bomber landed in the pig lot sparing the animals living there, there was one pig that died later. Its death was attributed to something left from the crash that the pig ingested. The government reimbursed Mr. Goad for the loss of his pig.

## The Crash: Fact or Fiction?

Sorting fact from fiction is one of the many challenges inherent in writing about an historic event, especially when many primary sources are still alive. I say that with great respect for the memories and differing points-of-view of those individuals who contributed to the telling of this tale. With that in mind, I'd like to clear up a few things:

## Myth # 1: The Plane:

The book itself has cleared up this myth but I mention it because among those that remembered the crash, the discussion still persists. Aaron McAlexander said, "I must have heard ten different versions of what kind of plane it was from a C-47 to a B-29."[93]

Identifying aircraft had become a hobby, especially among children living in the area, because singular military aircraft or squadrons flew over Meadows of Dan and Floyd and Willis several times a day. The February 2, 1942 issue of Life Magazine published an article displaying the silhouettes of the different American war planes and encouraged every American to learn to recognize them.[94] The children memorized them all, making great sport out of seeing who could identify the most and sparking debates over who was right and who was wrong.

## Myth #2: The Wedding Dress:

When Capt. Streadbeck was rescued by the Barnard family, he walked through the door and handed sixteen-year old Jesse his parachute and told her to make a wedding dress out of it. From that comment a great romantic tale was spun about how the Captain came back after the war and years later married Jesse. This was a fairy tale.

Additional people still believe a wedding dress was made and worn.

The truth is Jesse had a brother, William Barnard, who was in the Army Air Corp, serving stateside. When William came home on leave he saw the parachute and told the family they couldn't keep it. So Jesse's father packed it in a box and sent it back to Lockbourne Army Air force base.

## Myth #3: Rescuing 1st Lt. Hobin:

According to legend, the pilot who broke his leg landed in a tree and several men took part in the rescue. I had the pleasure of speaking with now 99-year old Major Hobin and he told me, as reported in the Bailing Out Chapter, that the nighttime fog was so dense he never saw the ground until he hit it.

This myth may have grown out of the fact that the terrain where the four pilots landed was mountainous and several men, along with the doctor, did aid in finding and rescuing Pfc. Poore, 1st Lt. Hall and 1st Lt. Hobin while 1st Lt. Grimson anxiously awaited their return at the farmhouse.

## Myth #4: Engines in the swamp:

The myth persists that there are engines, anywhere from one to three of them, still buried in the muddy swamp. As was reported earlier in the story by Arlie Dalton, grandson of the Goad's living on the property at the time, three of the engines were excavated and the fourth one found behind a clump of bushes. There are no engines still in the swamp anymore.

**Finding a piece of *The Spirit of South High:***

The portion of the property where the crash occurred was sold to the National Park System before Mr. Goad's death three years after the crash. His widow maintained the farm as best she could and was allowed to stay in her house until her death. Nothing has been done with the land since. The property where the crash occurred has been virtually untouched for almost seventy years.

On May 3, 2015, my husband, Roger and I, along with John Reynolds, Historian from the Patrick County Historical Society visited the crash site. While walking the property that day, John saw the reflection of a shiny object peeking out from under some leaves. He reached down and picked it up. Barely visible to us were a few letters and numbers that had been etched on its side. Roger guessed the combination, plugged the numbers into his smart phone and up came the following information:

WWII USAAF Aviation Plug Socket!

We had found a piece of *The Spirit of South High*! The part is being cleaned and catalogued by archivists from the Blue Ridge Parkway and will be placed on loan with the Patrick County Historical Society, the county in which Meadows of Dan and the crash site resides.

WWII USAAF aviation plug socket FOUND by John Reynolds, May 3, 2015, at the crash site, Meadows of Dan, Virginia.

*Photos by Sandra Warren, May 3, 2015*

## South High School: The Spirit Lives On:

The year 2015, marks the 100th year anniversary of the opening of South High School and the forty-seventh year of its closing. In 2021, South High School will have been closed as many years as it had been open, fifty-three years. And yet the spirit lives on.

What seems improbable is that as of this date, 2015:

- Twenty-seven years after the closing of South High, in 1995, a South High School Scholarship fund was established that yearly presents two scholarships for books and tuition for "C" students to attend Grand Rapids Jr. College.

- Over one-hundred former South High athletes, all members of the Varsity Club, still meet once a year to celebrate old victories!

- A monthly breakfast for alums is held at the New Beginnings Restaurant on the north end of Grand Rapids!

- The last Tuesday of every month alums can attend a luncheon hosted by 1957 South High School graduate, Marge Wilson at Marge's Donut Den in Wyoming, Michigan.

- Marge also hosts a South High School All-School reunion once a year outside her establishment, Marge's Donut Den.

South High School was not perfect. It was not a wealthy school. The majority of students came from factory working families. Well-integrated, the school was a microcosm and as such reflected the good as well as the not so good that society offers. But in this author's opinion, having attended the school for six years, South High School represented the way life should be, multi-cultures living and working together in mutual respect and harmony.

## Searching for the *SPIRIT* that is South High School:

What is it about a school that keeps it alive fifty years after its closing?

Where does that spirit come from?

The search for answers to that question ignited the spark that propelled the writing of this book.

In 2012, for the fiftieth reunion of the Class of 1962, I compiled a history of South High that I called, "Searching for the Spirit" never dreaming that it would bring me to this moment. After that presentation former classmate, Joe Rogers, overheard a comment I made about the "Buy a Bomber" story that piqued his curiosity. He searched military websites on the Internet and found a crash report for a B-17 bomber serial number 42-29577.

At long last, Joe and I had proof, *The Spirit of South High* had been found.

It was time to tell the rest of the story.

# APPENDIX

The United States Army Air Force Nose Art Research Project maintains a list of all the businesses, organizations, municipalities and schools that participated in the War Bond funding drive called the "Buy a Bomber" campaign.

If you are aware of additional unlisted entities who participated or you have photos to augment an existing listing, please contact Ray Bowden rjbowden@freenetname.co.uk. Or visit the website http://tinyurl.com/kdxpxwk.

## CHART OF WAR BOND AIRCRAFT PURCHASE

### War Bond Aircraft    War Bond Contributor

| War Bond Aircraft | War Bond Contributor |
|---|---|
| B-24J | A.B. Davis High School, Mt. Vernon (?) |
| P-51 | Amarillo-Employees of N. American Aviation Co. |
| B-17G | American Serbian (?) |
| B-25 | American Syrian Lebanese of W. VA |
| P-47 or P-40 | Citizens of Andrew County, MO |
| L-5B | Angel of Mercy Students of Parkman School, Detroit, MI |
| L-5 | Angel of Mercy Students of Greusel Intermediate, Detroit, MI |
| L-5 | Angel of Mercy Students of Burns Elementary, Detroit, MI |
| P-51 | Athens Golden Eagles Citizens of Athens, Georgia |
| P-40, P47, P51 | The Avenger Phelps Co. Citizens of Phelps County, MO |
| B-17 | The Bataan Sheboygan County, WI |
| P-51 | The Bengal Lancer Students of Bloomfield High School, NJ |
| B-24J | Big Boy 1000th plane through Bechtel-McCone-Parsons Corp |
| B-17 | Bomberlin Federal Employees of Cleveland |
| P-47 or P-40 | Borough Of Hellerton Citizens, Northampton County, PA |
| B-17G | Brass City Kitty Citizens of Waterbury, New Haven County, CT |
| L-5 | Bring Em Back Alive Students of Highland Park Jr. High, Detroit, MI |
| B-14 or B-24 | United Service Women, Butler County, Iowa |
| L-5 | Bryan J. Rivett Students of Northwestern High School, Detroit, MI |
| P-40 or P-47 or P-51 | Camden County, MO |
| B-17 | Citizens of Cameron County, TX |
| B-25 | Am. Legion Posts #7, & Manning, Coon Rapids & Carroll County, IA |
| B-17 or B-24 | Am. Legion Post, Carroll County, IA |
| B-24 or B-17 | "Demon" Cass County, MO |
| B-24 or B-17 | "Raider" Cass County, MO |
| P-47 or P-40 or P-51 | Citizens of The Challenger Co. Phelps County, MO |

118

## War Bond Aircraft    War Bond Contributor

| War Bond Aircraft | War Bond Contributor |
|---|---|
| B-24 | Cherryot, Citizens of Traverse County, MI |
| B-17 or B-24 | Chester, Upper Darby Delaware County |
| B-17 or B-24 | Citizens of Alton, IL |
| B-17F | Citizens of Amarillo, TX |
| B-17 or B-24 | Citizens of Beaumont (?) |
| B-17 or B-24 | Citizens of Burlingame, CA |
| B-24 or B-27 or B-29 | City of Carthage, MO |
| B-17F | Citizens of Centralia, IL |
| B-17 | Citizens of Chester  (?) |
| P-51 | Citizens of Clovis, New Mexico |
| B-17 | Citizens of Danville, VA |
| P-47D | Citizens of Healdsburg, CA |
| B-24D | Citizens of Fort Worth |
| B-17G | Citizens of Lima |
| B-17 or B-24 | Supreme Moose Lodge, City of Mooseheart |
| B-17 or B-24 | Citizens of Cities of Beaumont, Port Arthur & Neches |
| B-25 | Citizens of Reno |
| P-51 | Citizens of Roswell, New Mexico |
| B-17 | City of Ruston "Women at Work Week" |
| B-17 or B-24 | Bomber for MacArthur Campaign, City of Toledo |
| B-17 or B-24 | City of Troy, NY |
| B-24 | Citizens of Waco, TX |
| B-24 or B-17 or B-24 | Citizens of Webb City, MO |
| B-24 | Citizens of Wyandotte, MI |
| I-5 | Cleveland Mercy Ship, Citizens of Tarrant County, TX |
| B-24 or B-17 | Citizens of Clinton County, MO |
| P-51 | The Comet Students of Hackensack High School, Hackensack, NJ |
| L-5 or Hospital a/c | Citizens of St. Clair County, MO |
| P-51 | Employees of North American Aviation Co., Corpus Christi, TX |
| B-24D | Citizens of Tarrant County, TX |
| B-17 or B-24 | Coyote Phoenix Union High School |
| B-17 or B-24 | Croatian Fraternal Union |
| P-40 or P-47 or P-51 | Citizens of Dade County, MO |
| P-47 | Citizens of Dawson County, Nebraska |
| L-5 or C-47 or Hospital a/c | Citizens of De Kalb County, MO |
| B-25 | Detroit Chap. Of Hadassan, Women's Organization, Detroit, MI |
| P-47 | Citizens & pupils of Florida Schools, Amatilla & Nicaragua |
| B-17 | Citizens of Franklin County, MS |
| P-47 | Citizens of Freedonia, OH |
| B-17 or B-24 | Gage County Sod Busters, Citizens of Gage County, (?) |
| B-25 | Gun City Gal Citizens of Watervliet, (?) |
| B-17 or B-24 | Ha-Da-Ska Oklahoma Ottawa County 4-H Clubs |
| L-5 | Headin Home Donated by Employees of Chrysler Corporation |
| B-17F | Citizens of Hildalgo, TX |
| L-5 | High Flyer Students of University High School, Ann Arbor, MI |

# War Bond Aircraft    War Bond Contributor

| | |
|---|---|
| B-17F | Members of Farm Bureau Federation of Breenville, MS |
| A-20 or B-25 or B-2 | Citizens of Howard County, MO |
| B-17F | Citizens of Idalou County, TX |
| P-47 | Citizens of Jackson County, MI |
| B-17F | Citizens of Jasper County, MO |
| B-17 or B-24 | Citizens of Beaumont, Jefferson County (?) |
| B-24 or B-17 | Citizens of Joplin, Jasper County MO |
| B-24 | Citizens of Joplin, Jasper County MO |
| P-51 | The Joplin School System, Citizens & Pupils, Joplin, MO  + 5 Jeeps |
| B-17 or B-24 | Woman's City Club of Panama City 3rd War Loan Drive |
| B-17F | Members of Mississippi Farm Bureau Federation, Kemper County |
| A-20 or B-25 or B-26 | Citizens of Knox County Missouri |
| B-17F | Members of Lafayette Mississippi Farm Bureau, Lafayette County |
| B-24-FO | Employees of Lear Avia, Inc., Piqua, Christined in Detroit |
| B-17F | Citizens of Lewis County Washington |
| L-5 or C-47 or Hospital a/c | Citizens of St. Charles County, MO |
| B-25 | Citizens of Lodi, San Joaquin County, CA |
| P-40 | Refugees from Nazis - Christened at LaGuardia Field |
| P-51 | Lubbock County, Lubbock City Federation of Women's Clubs |
| B-25 or B-26 | Citizens of Macon County, MO |
| B-24 | Citizens of Manitee County, MI |
| B-24H - 15DT | Manistee |
| A-20 or B-25 or B-2 | Citizens of Marion County, MO |
| P-47 or P-40 | Citizens of McDonald County, MO |
| B-25 | Students of McKinley Junior High School, Muncie, IN |
| P-47 or P-40 | Citizens of Mercer County, WVA |
| B-24 | Citizens of Mercer County, WVA |
| B-17F | Citizens of Brazoria County, TX (1942) |
| B-17F | Citizens of Brazoria County, TX (1943) |
| P-40 or P-47 or P-51 | Citizens of Dallas County, MO |
| B-17 or B-24 | Gaston County Women's Division, Gastonia, NC |
| B-25 | Citizens of Kileen, Bell County, TX |
| Trainer | Morton School, West Lafayette, IN |
| B-24 or B-17 | Citizens of Neosho County, MO |
| B-25 | Maryville Business & Professional Women's Club, Maryville, MO |
| B-17G - 1-VE | 9000 War Bond Buyers at MT, MN, ND, WI, IA |
| B-24 | Oakland County, MI |
| P-47 | Oregon's Britannia |
| B-24 or B-17 | Citizens of Ozark, Christian County, MO |
| B-17G | Federation of Women's Clubs, Panama City |
| B-25 | Susanville Elks Lodge No. 1487 |
| B-24 | Clipper -Employees of Peerless Woollen Mills, Chattanooga, TN |
| B-24 | Clipper-II-Employees of Peerless Woollen Mills, Chattanooga, TN |
| P-40 or P-47 or P-51 | Citizens of Camden County, MO |

## War Bond Aircraft    War Bond Contributor

| War Bond Aircraft | War Bond Contributor |
|---|---|
| P-47 or P-51 | Members of Phoenix Lioness Club |
| B-24 or B-17 | Citizens of Phelps, MO |
| B-24 (?) | Citizens of Pique, OH |
| P-51 | Plover Iowa Tiger |
| P-51 | Plover Iowa Tiger |
| B-17F | Employees of Trojan Powder Co. Sandusky, OH |
| B-24D | Polish Community of Franklin County, MA |
| B-24 or B-17 | Citizens of Adair County, MO |
| B-17F | Citizens of Dunklin County, MO |
| B-17F | Members Mississippi Farm Bureau Federation, Jasper County, MS |
| A20-or B-25 or B-26 | Citizens of Laclede County, MO |
| P-47 or P-40 | Citizens of Madison County, MO |
| A20-or B-25 or B-26 | Citizens of McDonald County, MO |
| P-40 or P-47 or P-51 | Citizens of Osage County, MO |
| P-40 or P-47 or P-51 | Citizens of Ozark County, MO |
| A-20 or B-25 or B-26 | Citizens of Scotland County, MO |
| P-40 or P-47 or P-51 | Citizens of Sullivan County, MO |
| B-17 | Citizens of Twin Falls, ID |
| B-25 | Citizens of Watervliet |
| P-47 | Employees of Republic Aviation Corporation |
| P-47 | Citizens of Redondo Beach, CA |
| P-47 | Citizens of Women's Division of Richland County War Loan Drive |
| Unknown | Members of Rodel Shalom Sisterhood & B'nai B'rith Congregation |
| P-51D - 10-NA | Rough Rider |
| B-25 | 1200 Employees of Overland Greyhound Bus Line |
| P-47 | Scarsdale Legionnaire Citizens of Scarsdale, NY |
| P-47 | Scarsdale Comet, Citizens of Scarsdale, NY |
| P-47 | Short Stuff war bond Aircraft |
| P-51 | Sikeston Schools, MO |
| V-17 | Order of Sons of American Lodges, Adam County, Gettsyburg, New Oxford and Littlestown, PA |
| B-17 or B-24 | Ohio's 4-H Youth Development Clubs |
| B-17G | Citizens of Allen County OH |
| B-25 | Citizens of Athens |
| P-47 | Citizens of Atlantic City, NJ |
| B-17 | Bataan Relief Organization, Kirkland Field, Albuquerque, NM |
| B-24 | Citizens of Memphis, TN |
| P-47 | Citizens of Bellflower, CA |
| B-24 | Beverly Hills Schools, Beverly Hills, CA |
| B-17F | Bloomfield New Jersey Schools, Bloomfield, NJ |
| B-17 or B-24 | Citizens of Brazoria County, TX |
| P-40 or P-47 or P-51 | Citizens of Clark County, MO |
| B-17 | Spirit of Cleveland, christened by Mrs. FJ Lausche |
| B-17 F | Members - Mississippi Farm Bureau Federation, Koahoma County |

# War Bond Aircraft    War Bond Contributor

| | |
|---|---|
| B-24 or B-17 | Citizens of Cole County, MO |
| B-17G | Citizens of Columbus, MS |
| B-24 | Students of Detroit Schools, Detroit, MI |
| P-47 | Citizens of Crawford County (?) |
| A-20 or B-25 or B-26 | Citizens of Davies County, MO |
| P-51C | Citizens of Binghampton, NY |
| B-17F | Citizens of Falmouth, MA |
| B-17F ??? | Citizens of Franklin County, MO |
| B-24 | Spirit of Hollywood |
| B-24 | Spirit of Illinois |
| B-24 | Citizens of Queens County, NY |
| B-24 | Employees of Jakes Associates |
| B-25 | Citizens of Limestone County, AL |
| A-20 or B-25 or B-26 | Citizens of Livingston County MO |
| P-47 | Los Angeles City College, Citizens of Los Angeles |
| B-24 | Massillion High School, Massillion, OH |
| P-51C | Citizens of Milwaukee, MI |
| P-47 | Citizens of Milwaukee County, Milwaukee, WI |
| P-51 | Citizens of Moniteau County, (?) |
| B-24 | Citizens of Montesano, Grays Harbor County, WA |
| B-24 | Spirit of Mt. Sinai, Detroit, MI |
| A-20 or B-25 or B-26 | Citizens of Osage County, MO |
| B-25 | Students of Cove & Panama Grammar Schools, Panama City, FL |
| B-24 | Citizens of Plainfield, NJ |
| 24D | Citizens of Pocohontas County, IA |
| B-25 | Citizens of Randolph County, Moberly, MO |
| P-51B (?) | Citizens of Richmond, MI |
| P-51 | Students of Sikeston Schools, MO |
| B-17F | Members of the South Carolina Pilots Clubs |
| B-17 F-60-BO | Students of South High School, Grand Rapids, MI |
| B-25 | Citizens of Sparks, NV |
| Unknown fighter | Inmates of Norfolk State Prison Colony |
| P-47 or P-40 | Citizens of St. Genevieve County, MO |
| B-25 | Spirit of Taft High School, Citizens of West Side |
| P-51D | Students of Tech High, Indianapolis, IN |
| B-17F-120-BO | Employees of Union Pacific Railways |
| P-51A | Employees of Universal Studios, Corporation |
| B-24 | Students of West Technical High School, Cleveland, OH |
| B-24 | Citizens of Ypsilanti, MI |
| P-51 | Citizens of St. Joseph, MO |
| B-24 | Florida War Savings Committee, Sunshine City, FL |
| B-25 or B-17 or B-2 | Citizens of Quaker Village, Swarthmore, PA |
| B-17F | Members of Mississippi Farm Bureau Federation, Tate County |
| P-51 | Citizens of Taylor County, IA |
| B-25 | Members of the Texas State Board of Beauticians |
| P-47 or P-40 | Citizens of Texas County, MO |

122

## War Bond Aircraft    War Bond Contributor

| | |
|---|---|
| B-25 | Members of Texas Federation of Women's Clubs (4th drive) |
| B-24 | Citizens of Alpena, MI (1st drive) |
| B-24 | Citizens of Alpena, MI  (2nd drive) |
| B-24J -10-DT | Employees of Douglas Aircraft Company |
| B-24H-10-FO | Citizens of Nashville, TN |
| B-17 or B-24 | Independent Order of Odd Fellows and the Rebekahs of Texas |
| P-51 | Employees of North American Aviation Co., Waco, TX |
| P-47 | Employees of Republic Aviation Corporation (1st drive) |
| P-47 | Employees of Republic Aviation Corporation (2nd drive) |
| B-17F | Members of Mississippi Farm Bureau Federation,  MS |
| A-20 or B-25 or B-2 | Citizens of Webster County, MO |
| P-51C | Employees of North American Aviation Co., Wichita Falls, TX |
| P-47 ? | Women of Birmingham, AL |
| P-51C | Yahooskin War Bond Drive a/c |

*Courtesy of Ray Bowden, USAAF-Nose Art*

The "Buy a Bomber" program wasn't the only funding campaign initiated by the United States Treasury Department to fund the war effort. Children were shown through their Weekly Reader: The Children's Newspaper and The Weekly Reader: The Junior Newspaper what even the smallest donation would purchase.

> One 10 cent stamp  -- Three Cartridges
> One 25 cent stamp – Feeds one Carrier Pigeon
> Twenty 25 cent stamps – One Steel Helmet
> Thirty-three $ 5.00 – One Army Horse
> $10.00 – One pair of Hickory Skis
> $18.75 -- One Winter Flying Jacket
> $18.75 –  One Walkie Talkie
> $37.50 – Two Small Operating Tables
> $1,000 – Bomb Trailer with a M-5
> $1,165 – Land Jeep
> $2,090 – Amphibian Jeep

$3,000 – Flying Jeep
$4,000 – Two Field Ambulances
$9,995 – One Barrage Balloon
$15,000 – One Pontoon Boat
$60,000 – Medium Tank with a 75mm Gun
$331.15 would purchase the following: One Sub-Machine Gun, Four Field Telephones, One Tent, Five Steel Helmets, Nine Entrenching Tools.

To put these amounts in perspective, here are the 2015 equivalents:

| **1943** | **2015** |
| --- | --- |
| 10 cents | $1.38 |
| 25 cents | $3.47 |
| $5.00 | $69.47 |
| $18.75 | $260.51 |
| $75,000 | $1,042,065.08 |
| $375,000 | $5,210,325.44 |

Resources: My Weekly Readers: The Children's Newspaper
November 16-November 20, 1942, No. 1
December 7-December 11,1942 No. 1
January 25-January 29, 1943, No. 1
Vol XXI, September 13-September, 1943 No. 1
Vol XXI, November 29-December 3, 1943 No. 11
Vol XXI, November 29-December 3, 1943 No. 11
Vol XXI, November 29-December 3, 1943 No. 11
Vol XXI, November 29-December 3, 1943 No. 11
Clinchfield School, Marion, North Carolina, Certificate from U.S Treasury Department, May 31, 1945.
Cruce, Ashley, "Working Papers-School Based Savings Program, 1930-2002, 02-07, February 2002, Washington University, St. Louis, Missouri, Page 15.

# ACKNOWLEDGEMENTS

From the beginning, in Michigan and Virginia, folks were eager to share their memories, expertise and knowledge about the events that transpired and the people involved. Not one word of this incredible story could have been told without the assistance of multiple people. I salute all of them and send my heartfelt thanks.

When Arthur Blackport raised his hand in Civics class he could never have predicted the turn of events it would precipitate. In an interview, Arthur admitted he surprised himself by speaking out. He didn't think it was that big a deal at the time. Thank you Arthur for instigating what became a history making accomplishment.

This book wouldn't have been written at all if my South High School classmate, Joe Rogers, hadn't been curious enough to hunt for aircraft number 42-29577 and then share the accident report he found with me. Thank you Joe! I couldn't have done it without you.

David Dutcher and his son, Doug Windsor, spent hours in interviews and acquiring the facts that I needed. As the Co-Chairmen of the "Buy a Bomber" committee, David had much to share. His collection of "South High School Tattler" newspapers, from 1943 and 1944, were invaluable.

Aviators Dick VanGemert, James Webb and Sean Elliot helped this non-aviator interpret the military report of the crash. Pilot Dick VanGemert, South High School Class of 1954, along with pilot James Webb, critiqued the "Trouble in the Sky" chapter from an aviator's point-of-view. Sean Elliot, a B-17 pilot with the Experimental Aviation Association (EAA) in Oskosh, Wisconsin, answered my questions specific to the B-17 Flying Fortress bomber. I am greatly indebted to all these men who helped me prove by surrounding myself with the right experts, I can write anything

Marge Wilson, South High School Class of 1957 graduate and owner of Marge's Donut Den, in Wyoming, Michigan, used her marketing skills to raise contributions to help with the publication of this project. Her love of South High School, reflected in enthusiasm for this project, helped bring it to fruition.

My heartfelt thanks also to the many who responded to Marge's call for support; Allen Gamble, Don & Helen Dieleman, Marge Wilson, Dan Warren, Loyce Johnson Kompar, Dan Humpfries, Leslie & Kyle Bauman and family, South High School Class of 1962 and the many South High Alumni who frequent Marge's Donut Den.

Classmate Leonard Esselink, worked up until the last minute helping secure photographs and gathering other miscellaneous information that I needed.

Allen Gamble, South High School Historian, researched old South High Spectra yearbooks and aided in finding folks to interview. Thanks to him also for helping me acquire an original "Minute Man Flag" for the school's museum.

Frank Russo, who maintains the South High School Facebook page, put the call out to find classmates to interview. Frank also works continuously to keep the South High Spirit alive.

Thank you to South High School 1943-1947 graduates, Betty DeStaffano Taber, Don Hondorp and Len Stormzand who shared memories of attending South High School during that period. Dean Wolf also shared memories of that time period.

I also owe the employees at the Grand Rapids Public Museum and the Grand Rapids Public Library a great deal of gratitude for assisting me in finding photographs. Andrea Melvin, Collections Curator at the Grand Rapids Public Museum located the photograph that was used on the cover of this book. She was instrumental in putting me in contact with Alex Forist and Michael Gillis, Editorial Administrator, MLive Media Group, owners of the Grand Rapids Press. Julie Tabberer and Sarah Scott of the Grand Rapids History and Special Collections Department of the Grand Rapids Public Library helped find copies of the photos of "Bomber

Day." Retired librarian Ellen Wood also aided in the search for information.

Row Luther, a Community Archives and Research Center Intern at the Grand Rapids Public Museum, assigned to the project, recognized the name of David Dutcher as a neighbor of her grandparents. She took it upon herself to interview David Dutcher and ultimately put me in contact with him. Without her contact, this book would not be as detailed. Claire and Dennis Naughton took time out of a visit to Grand Rapids to conduct research for me at the Gerald R. Ford Museum.

John Reynolds, Secretary, Patrick County Historical Society, Stuart, Virginia, embraced this project from the start when I called and asked about the crash of a WWII bomber that had been long forgotten. It was only fitting that he would be the one to find a piece of the bomber lying in the leaves as if waiting for us to awaken it and this story, seventy-one years later.

*The Enterprise* from Stuart, Virginia, and *The Martinsville Bulletin*, from Martinsville, Virginia, printed articles about my search for folks to interview who might remember the crash. Richard Rogers of radio station WHEO out of Stuart, Virginia broadcast an interview with me on his morning radio show that resulted in several contacts with local residents who had memories of the day the B-17 fell out of the sky.

I am indebted to the following Virginia residents who shared their memories in telephone interviews: Ruth Jean Bolt, Marie Terry Bowman, Patsy Cockram, Alfred and Dot Cruise, Armand Harrell, Aaron McAlexander, Vera Barnard Seigler and Mary Edith Goad Wade.

Arlie Eugene Burnette, Linda Fain and Arlie Dalton, met with me at Mabry's Mill to point out the exact location where *The Spirit of South High* crashed.

Vera Barnard Seigler invited me to her home, so I could walk the area, about five hundred feet from her house, where her father, A. M. Barnard, rescued Captain Streadbeck.

Linda Fain relayed additional information from her father and sent me additional newspaper articles.

Patsy Cockram, went out of her way to send me additional newspaper articles about the event.

When Felicia Shelor, from Poor's Farm Market, posted my request for information on the Poor's Farm Market Facebook page, the following folks responded: Jeff Dalton, Pat Galbraith, Dotty Griffith, Ruth Hall, LaNita Harris, Loreen Harris, Ruth Hall, Rex Ingram, Tom Perry, Leslie Shelor and Opal Webster. All their comments served to enhance my understanding of the Virginia side of the story. A few of their individual memories can be found within the pages of this book.

Blue Ridge Parkway officials, Steven Kidd, Jackie Holt and Mike Ryan were supportive of the project. Mike Ryan met with me, Arlie Burnette and Arlie Dalton when we toured the crash site, in early May. Karen Hall, author of several books about the Blue Ridge Parkway was also extremely helpful.

Librarian Patty Holda from the McDowell Public Library in Marion, North Carolina went out of her way to help me find information about "My Weekly Reader: The Junior Newspapers."

Many friends, family and even strangers lent their support:

Neighbor and Army Veteran William (Bill) Schumacher shared material on the B-17 bomber.

Barbara Alpert and Katherine House, two authors who frequent a non-fiction yahoo group on the Internet called, NFforkids, both offered advice in finding a particular copy of "My Weekly Reader: The Junior Newspaper," I was looking for. Although I was unable to find the copy I needed, I do appreciate their help.

Walker Carriker, a gentleman I met during Memorial Day festivities generously loaned six books, all personal accounts of different B-17 WWII pilots. These personal accounts enhanced my understanding of what the pilots on *The Spirit of South High* went through. The books were loaned from his extensive WWII collection.

Several friends helped edit the manuscript, some reading it three or four times. Thank you to my critique group, Debbie Allman, Teresa Fannin and Gretchen Griffith. I appreciate all you've done to make my writing shine.

Pilots Dick VanGemert and James Webb, who read the manuscript and tweaked it where it was needed. Also, Major Arval Streadbeck, now ninety-nine years young, and his son, Larry Streadbeck checked the aviation chapter for accuracy.

I can't forget fellow classmate, Phyllis Holloway Corner, who did the final edits for me and artist Tom Sjoerdsma who consulted and critiqued the cover design.

Thank you to Kimberly Rae and Brian Thigpen for the amazing job with cover design and setting up this book for publication.

Last but not least, to my husband, Roger, who not only helped edit the story, he lived it with me on a daily basis; through the ups and downs and the sheer joy of bringing this story to life, I give you my utmost love and appreciation.

*We Bought a WWII Bomber: The Untold Story of a Michigan High School, a B-17 Bomber and The Blue Ridge Parkway*, was a story begging to be told. It practically wrote itself. Often I felt as if I were just the messenger and not the author. Even so, I couldn't have done it alone. Thank you ALL for helping me deliver this incredible story and for keeping the Spirit of South High School alive!

*Sandra Dieleman Warren*
*South High School Class of 1962*

# BIBLIOGRAPHY

**Chapter One: WWII Home Front**

[1] Daggett, Stephen, Specialists in Defense Policy and Budgets, "Costs of Major U.S. Wars," Congressional Research Service, June 29, 2010.

[2] Harms, Richard H., Voil, Robert W., <u>Grand Rapids Goes to War: The 1940's Homefront</u>, Grand Rapids Historical Society, 1993, page 34.

[3] "My Weekly Reader: The Children's Newspaper," Vol. 19, June 1-5, 1942, No. 37.

[4] Ibid.

[5] "Uncle Sam Needs Boys & Girls," My Weekly Reader: The Children's Newspaper, Vol. 20, November 9 – 13, 1942, No. 9.

[6] "Children Can Help," My Weekly Reader: The Children's Newspaper, Vol. 19, June 19 – 23, 1942, No. 18, page 1.

**Chapter Two: The War Impacts South High School**

[7] Winter, David G., "Why and How Did South High School Close?" University of Michigan, based on public archival sources available in the Grand Rapids Public Library.

[8] "Government Takes Four Typewriters," The South High Tattler, Vol. 27, No. 9, January 28, 1943, page 1.

[8] "War Savings Are Minor But Noticeable," The South High Tattler, Vol. 27, No. 4, November 12, 1942, page 1.

[9] "War Savings Are Minor But Noticeable," The South High Tattler, Vol. 27, No. 4, November 12, 1942, page 1.

[10] "Gov't Metals Drive Gets Spectra Cuts," The South High Tattler, Vol. 27, No. 1, October 2, 1942, page 1.

[11] "Effect Of War On Shops Seen In New Work, Material-Lack," The South High Tattler, Vol. 27, No. 3, October 29, 1942, page 1.

[12] "Rationing Effects Felt in Cafeteria," The South High Tattle, Vol. 28, No. 1, October 7, 1943, page 1.

[13] "Rationing," Vol. 28, No. 8, The South High Tattler, December 23, 1943, page 3.
[14] "Senior Class Smallest in 22 Years," The South High Tattler, Vol. 28, No. 1, October 7, 1943, page 1.

## Chapter Three: The Instigator

[15] "America Shows What It Can Do," My Weekly Reader: The Junior Newspaper, Vol. 20, February 16 – 20, 1942, No. 22.
[16] Bowden, Ray, "Nose Art Themes, War Bond Aircraft" http://www.usaaf-noseart.co.uk/theme.php?theme=6&code=404R#.Wa4VvlViko
[17] Blackport, Arthur, Interviewed by Sandra Warren, Febuary1, 2013.

## Chapter Four: Igniting the Campaign

[18] Dutcher, David, Video interview by Sandra Warren and Leonard Esselink, June 2, 2015.
[19] "Seek $75,000 As Drive to Buy Bomber Begins," The South High Tattler, Vol. 27, No. 7, December 23, 1942, page 1.
[20] Hamm, Richard H., Viol, Robert W., Grand Rapids Goes to War: The 1940's Homefront, Grand Rapids Historical Society, Grand Rapids, MI, 1993, page 34.
[21] "Bomber Campaign Enthusiasm Rises As Students Urge Sales," The South High Tattler, Vol. 27, No. 8, January 14, 1943, page 1.
[22] "Students Purchase $200 in War Stamps to See "Buy a Bomber" Entertainment," The South High Tattler, Vol. 27, No. 7, December 23, 1942, page 3.
[23] "Reach $75,000 Bomber Goal in Two Months Now Seek $300,000 in Community Drive," The South High Tattler, Vol. 27, No. 11, February 26, 1943, page 1.
[24] "Statistical Abstract of the United States 1944-1945," United States. Foreign and Domestic Commerce, United States. Bureau of the Census, http://tinyurl.com/pj29gnx.

[25] "Reach $75,000 Bomber Goal in Two Months Now Seek $300,000 in Community Drive," The South High Tattler, Vol. 27, No. 11, February 26, 1943, page 1.

## Chapter Five: The Christening

[26] "Queen Chosen to Christen Bomber: To Release Six Balloons At Ceremony," The South High Tattler, Vol. 27, No. 13, March 25, 1943, page 1.
[27] "Mark Army Day With Bomber Ceremony, Air School Review," The Grand Rapids Press, April 6, 1943.

## Chapter Six: The Pledges Keep Coming

[28] "Mark Army Day With Bomber Ceremony, Air School Review," The Grand Rapids Press, April 6, 1943.
[29] "South's Radio Unit, Largest in City, Enlisted For Defense by Mr. Sirrine, Owner Operator," The South Tattler, Vol. 27, No. 16, page 3.

## Chapter Seven: School Year 1943-1944

[30] "South Reaches 90% Goal: Obtains Minute Man Flag," The South Tattler, Vol. 28, No. 3, November 4, 1943, page 1.
[31] "South Rallies to Bond Cause; Barge Fleet is Aim of Drive," The South High Tattler, Vol. 28, No.9, February 3, 1944, page 1.
[32] "Battle Boats in Peaceful Park: 1800 Cheer Christening of South's War Barges," The Grand Rapids Press, April, 1944.

## Chapter Eight: The Bomber and The President

[33] "Battle Boats in Peaceful Park: 1800 Cheer Christening of South's War Barges," The Grand Rapids Press, April, 1944.

## Chapter Eight: The Bomber and The President

[34] Winter, David G., "Why and How Did South High School Close?" University of Michigan, page 19.

[35] "A Bombshell: Sparta historian Tracks South High's WWII B-17," The Grand Rapids Press, Tuesday, April 16, 1991.

**Chapter Nine: Trouble In The Sky**

[36] B-17 Pilot Training Manual, www.stelzriede.com.

[37] Streadbeck, Capt. Arval, Interviewed by Sandra Warren, June 30, 2015.

[38] Poore, Pfc. Ralph L., War Department U.S. Army Air Force Report of Aircraft Accident, Lockbourne Army Air Base, Affidavit, State of Ohio, County of Franklin, 5 October 1944, Pfc. Poore, page 1.

[39] Grimson, 1st Lt.William V., War Department U.S. Army Air Force Report of Aircraft Accident, Statement, Lockbourne Army Air Base, 2 October 1944, 1st. Lt. Grimson, page 1.

[40] Streadbeck, Capt. Arval, War Department U.S. Army Air Force Report of Aircraft Accident, Lockbourne Army Air Base, 2 October 1944, Capt. Streadbeck, page 2.

[41] Fitchko, 1st Lt. Hearty., War Department U.S. Army Air Force Report of Aircraft Accident, Lockbourne Army Air Base, Statement, 2 October 1944, 1st Lt. Fitchko, page 1.

[42] Streadbeck, Capt. Arval, War Department U.S. Army Air Force Report of Aircraft Accident, Lockbourne Army Air Base, 2 October 1944, Capt. Streadbeck, page 2.

[43] Fitchko, 1st Lt. Hearty., War Department U.S. Army Air Force Report of Aircraft Accident, Lockbourne Army Air Base, Statement, 2 October 1944, 1st Lt. Fitchko, page 1.

[44] What is Feathering an Engine? By rotating the blades of a propeller along its axis air resistance is lessened. Used particularly when an engine needed to be shut down to resist drag as otherwise the propeller would windmill.
Http://www.398th.org/Research/398th_FAW.html#anchor_B-17andA/CTerms.

[45] Streadbeck, Capt. Arval, War Department U.S. Army Air Force Report of Aircraft Accident, Statement, Lockbourne Army Air Base, 2 October 1944, Capt. Streadbeck, page 3.

[46] Hobin, 1st Lt. W. Michael, Interviewed by Sandra Warren, June 1, 2015.

[47] Poore, Pfc. Ralph L., War Department U.S. Army Air Force Report of Aircraft Accident, Lockbourne Army Air Base,

Affidavit, State of Ohio, County of Franklin, 5 October 1944, Pfc. Poore, page 2.

[48] Streadbeck, Capt. Arval, War Department U.S. Army Air Force Report of Aircraft Accident, Statement, Lockbourne Army Air Base, 2 October 1944, Capt. Streadbeck, page 3.

## Chapter Ten: Bailing Out

[49] Hobin, 1st Lt. W. Michael, Interviewed by Sandra Warren, June 1, 2015.

[50] Ibid.

[51] Ftichko, 1st Lt. Hearty, War Department U.S. Army Air Force Report of Aircraft Accident, Statement, Lockbourne Army Air Base, 2 October 1944, 1st Lt. Fitchko, page 2.

[52] Streadbeck, Capt. Arval, Personal Account of event, October 1, 1944.

## Chapter Eleven: Rescued

[53] McAlexander, Aaron, The Last One Leaving Mayberry, page 171, Stonebridge Press, 2011.

[54] Dalton, Arlie, Interviewed by Sandra Warren, May 3, 2015.

[55] Wade, Mary Edith Goad, Interviewed by Sandra Warren, April 7, 2015.

[56] Dalton, Arlie, Interviewed by Sandra Warren, April 27, 2015.

[57] Fitchko 1st Lt, Hearty, War Department U.S. Army Air Force Report of Aircraft Accident, Statement, Lockbourne Army Air Base, 2 October 1944, 1st Lt. Fitchko, page 2.

[58] Seigler, Vera Barnard, Interviewed by Sandra Warren, March 11, 2015.

[59] Streadbeck, Capt. Arval, War Department U.S. Army Air Force Report of Aircraft Accident, Statement, Lockbourne Army Air Base, 2 October 1944, Capt. Streadbeck, page 3.

[60] Streadbeck, Arval, Interviewed by Sandra Warren, June 30, 2015.

[61] Hobin, 1st Lt. R. Michael, Letter interview with Sharon Hobin Kasow, June 10, 2015.

**Chapter Twelve: The Clean-Up**

[62] "Big Army Bomber Crashes In Floyd." by Anne George, Martinsville Daily Bulletin, October 3, 1944.

[63] "Wrecked Plane Being Salvaged," Martinsville Daily Bulletin, October 3, 1944.

[64] Dalton, Arlie, interviewed by Sandra Warren, May 3, 2015.

[65] Ibid.

[66] Ibid.

[67] Burnette, Arlie, interviewed by Linda Fain, April 18, 2015.

[68] Cruise, Alfred and Dot, Interviewed by Sandra Warren, April, 20,2015.

[69] Hopkins, Lorene D., sent to Sandra Warren, April 11, 2015.

[70] McAlexander, Aaron, The Last One Leaving Mayberry, page 171, Stonebridge Press, 2011.

**Chapter Thirteen: A Different Perspective**

[71]"Baxter, Andrea, "A bombshell: Sparta historian tracks South High's WWII B-17," The Grand Rapids Press, April 16, 1991.

[72] Hobin, Maj. W. Michael, Letter sent to Sandra Warren, June 10, 2015.

[73] Fitchko, Col. Hearty, Obituary, TribeLive Total Media, http://tinyurl.com/nt76gve.

**Author Notes: Tying Up Loose Ends**

[74] Streadbeck, Maj. Arval L., Email received by Sandra Warren via Larry Streadbeck, July 4, 2015.

[75] Makos, Adam, Alexander, Larry, A Higher Call, The Berkeley Publishing Group, 2012, page 96.

[76] "Reach $75,000 Bomber Goal in Two Months Now Seek $300,000 In Community Drive," The South High Tattler, Vo. 27, No. 11, February 26, 1943.

[77] Rogers, Joe, Email, Saturday, June 6, 2015.

[78] Bowden, Ray, USAAF Nose Art Research Project, http://tinyurl.com/pb2vqal.

[79] Ground Looped. In aviation, a ground loop is a rapid rotation of a fixed-wing aircraft in the horizontal plane while on the ground. Aerodynamic forces may cause the advancing wing to rise, which may then cause the other wingtip to touch the ground. www.Wikipedia.com.

[80] Plaunt, 2nd Lt. James A., War Department US Army Air Forces Report of Aircraft Accident, 27, September, 1944, page 4.

[81] Harms, Richard H. and Viol, Robert W., Grand Rapids Goes To War: The 1940's Homefront, Grand Rapids Historical Society, 1993, page 39.

[82] Bowden, Ray, USAAF Nose Art Research Project, http://www.usaaf-noseart.co.uk

[83] Ibid.

[84] "America Shows What It Can Do," My Weekly Reader: The Junior Newspaper, Vol. 20, Week of February 16-20, 1942, No. 22.

[85] Shelor, Leslie, Email received, April 1, 2015.

[86] Dalton, Arlie, Interviewed by Sandra Warren, May 3, 2015.

[87] Bowman, Marie Terry, Interviewed by Sandra Warren, April 20, 2015.

[88] McAlexander, Aaron, Interviewed by Sandra Warren, March 20, 2015.

[89] Seigler, Vera Barnard, Interviewed by Sandra Warren, April 11, 2015.

[90] McAlexander, Aaron, <u>The Last One Leaving Mayberry</u>, Stonebridge Press, 2011, page 172.
[91] Cockram, Patsy, Interviewed by Sandra Warren, April 9, 2015.
[92] Bowman, Marie Terry, Interviewed by Sandra Warren, April 20, 2015.
[93] McAlexander, Aaron, Interviewed by Sandra Warren, March 20, 2015.
[94] Ibid.

**Websites:**

http://www/aviationarchaeology.com. List of military crashes in US in Oct. 1944.
http://www.faa.gov/air_traffic/flight_info/avn/flightinspection/fihistory. Explanation of aerial
navigation in the 1940's.
http://aviation.about.com/od/Navigation-Advances/a/Air-Navigation.htm, How Do Pilots Navigate, by Sarina Houston Aviation & Aerospace Expert.
http://www.398th.org/Research/398th_FAQ.html#anchor_B-17andA/CTerms, FAQs about Army Air Force Terms in WWII, B-17 and General Aircraft Terms FAQs, Mission Related FAQs.http://www.398th.org/History/Veterans/Voices/Transcriptions/Interview_Petrocine_Pep.html#PP_Feathering. Information about feathering.
http://www.adlit.org/unlocking_the_past/glossary_of_terms/, Unlocking the past - Glossary of World War II Vocabulary and Concepts (European Theatre).

http://tinyurl.com/p2jzd5s URL associated with WWII posters of the SCRAP DRIVE related to rationing and collecting scrap to use for military equipment; shoes, clothing, guns, bombers, tanks, etc.

http://www.usaaf-noseart.co.uk/theme.php?theme=6&code=404R#.Wa4VvlViko

Information and list of "Buy a Bomber" campaign participants.
Ray Bowden

http://www.aviationarchaeology.com/src/AARmonthly/Sep1944S.ht
Crash of small fighter plane 4115903.

http://www.savingsbonds.com/bond_basics/series-e-savings-
bonds.cfm
Info about savings bond maturity rates.

http://en.wikipedia.org/wiki/North_American_T-6_Texan
Link to information on the AT-6A Texan Trainer fighter plane.


**Photographs Courtesy of:**
    Collections at Smithsonian Institute, Washington DC
    Gerald R. Ford Presidential Library
    Grand Rapids History & Special Collections, Archives, Grand
        Rapids Public Library, Grand Rapids, Michigan
    National Park Service, Blue Ridge Parkway
    South High School Spectra yearbooks 1943 – 1944
    The Grand Rapids Public Museum.
    National WWII Museum

**Personal Photographs Courtesy of:**
    W.Michael Hobin
    Arval L. Streadbeck
    Leonard Esselink
    Roger Warren
    Sandra Warren

**Cover Courtesy of:**
    The Grand Rapids Public Museum.

ABOUT THE AUTHOR:

Sandra Warren is a writer with publishing credits in multiple genres. She's written two additional military related stories; the biographies of two nurses who served in the Persian Gulf War. She lives and writes in a log home in the North Carolina Mountains.

Other works can be viewed on her website,
www.sandrawarren.com.

For Presentations, Book Talks, Skype Sessions or School visits,
www.sandrawarren.com/contact.htm